Notebooks of Elizabeth Cook-Lynn

Notebooks of Elizabeth Cook-Lynn

ELIZABETH COOK-LYNN

The University of Arizona Press
Tucson

The University of Arizona Press

© 2007 by Elizabeth Cook-Lynn

Library of Congress Cataloging-in-Publication Data
Cook-Lynn, Elizabeth.
  Notebooks of Elizabeth Cook-Lynn / Elizabeth Cook-Lynn.
    p. cm. — (Sun tracks ; v. 59)
  A brief collection of previously unpublished poetry and
political commentary from the desk of Elizabeth Cook-Lynn.
  ISBN-13: 978-0-8165-2583-6 (pbk. : acid-free paper)
  ISBN-10: 0-8165-2583-8 (pbk. : acid-free paper)
  1. Cook-Lynn, Elizabeth—Notebooks, sketchbooks, etc.
  I. Title. II. Series.
  PS3553.O5548N67 2007
  811´.54—dc22   2006017563

Publication of this book is made possible in part by
the proceeds of a permanent endowment created with
the assistance of a Challenge Grant from the National
Endowment for the Humanities, a federal agency.

Manufactured in the United States of America on acid-free,
archival-quality paper containing a minimum of 50% post-
consumer waste and processed chlorine free.

12 11 10 09 08 07   6 5 4 3 2 1

This collection of casual writings is dedicated to
all those who have *classified* the Native Races—
circa 1660 to the present—
making sounds that haunt us all the rest of our days.

Contents

Preface

I was living with relatives in a one-room tar-papered house on the Crow Creek Sioux Indian Reservation in South Dakota when I learned to read English, and as soon as I learned to read I wanted to write. The time was later called the dirty thirties, but, for me, it was a time marking the beginning of my interest in books. It took many decades for me to learn to use English efficiently. I published nothing until I was forty.

There was little to share except our lives in those early days because great holes of poverty and preferred silence were all around. With the exception of a grandmother and a sister just a year older than I, there was no one to share my grand thoughts with had they somehow mysteriously arisen. I have forgotten very little of what went on then, ordinary things like the ice breaking up on the creek in the spring and astonishing things like a friend of my father killing his wife and mother-in-law, his being hunted for days, weeks even, and our fear that he would come to our place for refuge out there in the middle of nowhere. What we didn't know was that minutes after he shot those he loved, he had gone into the woods a mile from his place and had ended it with the 30-30 he had borrowed from my father. His name was J. Long Turkey and he was a Santee and a relative of my grandmother's. There was no long ceremonial that followed this tragedy as there often was in other circumstances. Indeed, no one ever spoke of it.

A faded red pickup always sat in our yard and we started it up once in a while when we had gas money, and my grandfather taught me how to drive when I was six or seven. Perched on his lap, too small to reach the pedals, I learned how to shift gears, good skills for a child of two worlds. I've been shifting gears ever since. My grandpa, a grand-nephew of Bowed Head, who they say fought at the Little Big Horn with Sitting Bull and Gall, rode a bay mare to the Agency almost every day, a distance of about fourteen miles, sometimes even in winter snowstorms. He was a politician, a great "bull shitter," my father used to say, but I prefer to think of him as an Orator, a bilingual keeper of history. From him and others like him, I learned to value and honor words in two languages.

When I went to school, I copied poems on scraps of paper as soon as I saw them in books, not having any idea what they meant, not having mentors to "explicate" them for me. I remember copying and keeping "Thanatopsis" in my precious collection of writings, not knowing it was a poem about Death, the realm my grandmother taught me was sacred and not to be talked about. Even then and in the subsequent years that are supposed to bring about the philosophic mind, I continue to be bewildered by the neoclassicist tradition just as I am by the fables of the illiterate. The mystery of it all, though, has taught me that whatever is sought by wise men and women must be approached through Art.

I ∂∂∂

What about ART?

We ordinarily have a high regard for ART though sometimes we are reminded that accidental "masterpieces" are often called that simply because of the improbable taste of passersby, innocents, and sycophants. Thus, it is sometimes difficult to find masterpieces and even more difficult to know them when you see them. Just looking at, collecting, and financing doesn't tell us everything.

While driving past the Crazy Horse Monument in the Black Hills of South Dakota, one is reminded that this white-man's notion of ART, where thousands of tourists come every year is, alas, not Machu Picchu, also a well-trodden place by the daily influx of visitors. Not knowing the difference between Inca ruins and the white man's effort to seize the holy lands of the Sioux, tourists are witness to the blowing up of a sacred mountain. They see the fashioning of a false image of desolate, controlled, and expanding colonization, with little mention of the true history of the Man and his People whose desire it was to flourish and practice a tribal way of life. This image does not speak profoundly of the possibilities of the imagination and probably raises more questions about the function of the imagination than it answers. Is it a shrine? A cenotaph? Is it a monument? A temple? IS IT ART?

Monuments like Crazy Horse Monument, those pedestals where models of virtue are placed, hold none of the mysteries of ART, none of the enigmas, none of the ubiquitous questions of an indigenous people's sacred knowledge expressed for thousands of years in ways both realistic and unfathomable.

The stonework of Machu Picchu, on the other hand, is impressive, conveying the intimate relationship between a People and their surroundings, the shapes and spaces of the mountain landscape that the People venerated. This was also a holy place for the Inca Indians of Peru to imagine who they were and who they had always been. The worship of the sun took place here and great offerings were made. It was the last refuge, *a place never visited by the Spaniards.* There is no evidence of postconquest occupation at Machu Picchu, and, for some, that's what makes it a masterpiece called Art.

After we have seen a work, and have moved away from it, we take from it only the Memory of it. We remember that we have glimpsed something remarkable and we try to learn from it, how to live and die, how to conceive of our own personal existences. The visual language, obscure carvings that mark the places of Machu Picchu as special, presents the patterns and concepts still evident in the Inca ART portfolios and provides an understanding of culture. Thinking about that makes us ask the ultimate question about Art and the Imagination. What is the Memory of the Crazy Horse Monument we take with us when we drive on?

When we talk of

history, myth, identity, and art we are going back to origins. In what may be called the Native American Experience, there are historical and mythic journeys everywhere. To go back to origins it is suggested that we recognize the importance of geography; by that I mean a specific landscape so often referred to vaguely in lit/crit speak as a "sense of place." And we recognize the importance of language and we recognize the presence of those we call the holy people and we recognize all of the creature worlds, sights, and sounds of the universe that surround us as human beings and our lives. It is an astonishing thing to ponder, especially if you are an artist, not just those artists who sculpt or paint or sing, but those who write and tell the stories, too.

It seems to me that in terms of the imaginative concepts evident in Indian narratives, origin myths and historical migrations toward humanity are probably the least accessible and least well known of the influences. Yet those are the influences that resonate in the most humble of stories and poems.

A little piece I published some years ago illustrates this point, and it is retold in the following paragraphs. It is taken from one of my first significant publications in fiction, a 1990 collection of short stories published with Arcade. This is a collection of thirteen stories out of print for the last decade but recently reissued by the University of Arizona Press.

The collection is called *The Power of Horses and Other Stories*, but ... don't get the impression it is about horses. It isn't. It is about history, myth, and the secret journey toward humanity.

This collection begins with a brief story called "Mahpiyato," a kind of preface, or introduction. While you read it, try to think of "origins," try to think of geography and language and the holy people who might be known in Dakotah Sioux Mythology.

One late summer day the old woman and her grandchild walked quietly along the road toward the river, as they had done all their lives. The (k)unchi had a large soft blanket tied around her waist and shoulders, and the child swung two small pails, and so, those who might have noticed them knew that they were going to pick wild fruit. The blanket would be thrown beneath buffalo berry bushes to catch the small red fruit as the child, climbing high, would shake the branches vigorously. The small pails would hold the larger tart, wild plums.

The (k)unchi wore a black silk kerchief over her white hair, and as she walked, she pulled it closer over her forehead to shade her eyes from the intermittent sun. She shaded her eyes, also, with a slender hand as she looked up into the sky, and the child, attentive to every movement, followed her glance.

The great expanse of the river was shining before them, but, because of a cloud moving across the watery landscape, part of the river looked blue and the other part of it appeared to be dark gray where the shadow of the cloud fell upon it.

"Look at that!" the grandmother said softly in Indian language. And she stood still for a few moments, the child at her side.

"Look, *hunh-hu-hee-e-e-e*," indicating by the sound of her voice that a sober and interesting phenomenon was taking place right before their eyes. The child, a steadfast and modest companion of the old woman, knew from long experience about the moments when the stories came on and watched cautiously, leaning to one side so as to not catch the full glare in her eyes.

"That is what we call *mahpiyato*, isn't it?" said the old woman to the child.

"That is what *mahpiyato* really means." She stood as if entranced, her long fingers now touching the fringes of the blanket.

"To just say 'blue' or 'sky' or 'cloud' in English, you see, doesn't mean much. But *mahpiyato* is that Dakotah word which tells us what we are witnessing right now, at this very moment."

She pointed.

"You see, she is blue. And she is gray. *Mahpiyato* is, you see, one of the Creators. Look! Look! *Look at Mahpiyato!*"

Her voice was low and soft and very convincing.

That is the story. It seems simple enough. Yet it makes us ask: how is this kind of storytelling called Art? How does this storytelling assist in helping us to understand what Art does, what the imaginative concepts concerning origins may mean to this storyteller? Like the stonework of the Inca builder, the story, itself, suggests an indigenous understanding of holy places, the worship of the Sun, the last refuge.

The Journey into humanity, you see, for Dakotahs, often originates in Myth, even the little journey of the grandmother and the child going to the river to pick berries, which, on the face of it, seems a mundane and/or unremarkable event. Yet if we accept the notion that ideas and concepts of origin are essential elements of an indigenous text, we are required as readers to look more deeply into the cultural translations such a story presents. What the grandmother and the child have glimpsed is something remarkable. They will learn from it, how to live and die, how to conceive of their own personal existences.

It is important, then, for the storyteller and the listener to accept the Dakota Sioux mythic idea that Creators, sometimes thought of as the Holy Persons, are everywhere, and ever present in Dakotah thought systems and language, and experience.

The recording of native views while investigating philosophical formulations has always been the purpose of Dakota storytelling, especially that storytelling that tells one generation of listeners what the previous generation has come to know through the long tenancy of the tribe in a specific geography. This reality distinguishes "indigenous" storytelling from other more modern categories of storytelling. In this case, the grandmother, knowing what she knows about the universe and the river, articulates the phenomenon of sky and cloud behavior so that the symbiotic relationship between the universe and human beings is an accepted theory of humanness, that is, what it means to be human. The grandmother describes the sky and cloud formulations as human behaviors, making them feminine, communicating that the ever-changing sky relates those changes to the Dakotah persons standing on the earth as mere observers. The Dakota concept of sky behavior suggests a close relationship between humans and the Holy Persons (deities), even though the sky has existed as a holy being from the near beginnings of the Dakota universe even long before Dakotahs knew the Earth. Thus, the phenomenon is deserving of the awestruck attitude of mere humans; *hunh-hu-hee-e-e-e*, she says, an expression of wonder. It is a wonder to stand on the Earth and observe the behavior of what surrounds us.

It is an unfortunate reality that the study of American Indian Literatures today, with few exceptions, reveals that the new Indian Story being told in the mainstream is rarely believed to be the bearer of traditional knowledge, history, or myth. Perhaps we should not expect that this contemporary genre called Native American Literatures should be all of that or any of it since many American Indian writers today are not the practicing singers and chanters, tribal ritualists, medicine healers, not even committed participants in what may be called a tribal world. Often, these writers of the new American Indian story are not even the "informants" so ubiquitous in past and present anthropological studies and, so, they are by and large not well versed in the asserted knowledge available through ceremonial or ritual or tradition, or tribal language. What these writers are good at is telling stories, writing novels, practicing poetry and drama, writing memoirs and essays, making movies, and doing journalism; and they have produced in the past three decades a burst of self-interpretation that has astonished the literary world, starting with Momaday in 1968. It is the way of the present literary scene and has been an achievement of eminently readable works.

Whatever we need to say about origin stories is that the myths of origin and historical migration stories of the tribes remain the stuff of tradition in the new narrative and, ultimately, are what we rely on when we talk of identity. How does one say, "I am a Dakotah Sioux," or "Hopi," or "Dine"? That is the essential question.

Not long ago I listened to a cultural storytelling event given by a practicing practitioner of the Navajo tribes, and presenter of the Dine Hataa _ii Association. His name was Anthony Lee Sr., and he told of the significance of the Twin Warriors of Navajo mythology and its impact on Dine society today. He told of the birth of the Twins and how they grew up in a significant place (geography), to destroy what may be called in English "the evil Monsters." We recognize that the Twins, sometimes referred to as the duality in native thought, are everywhere in the indigenous stories. Mr. Lee's suggestion was that such knowledge assists modern Dine people (the Navajo) in understanding the contemporary issues faced by the people today, and certainly that duality shapes all intellectual and artistic activities in native communities still. Duality in all things, in all presences . . . male/female . . . good/evil . . . this world/the upper world.

If you are a Lakota/Dakota sundancer, for example, you recognize that duality in the sacred tree used as the essential object in ceremony and ritual. The cottonwood tree must be carefully chosen with a fork in it about halfway up, and in its limbs it carries the perfect star signifying the beginning of time.

Native Literatures are replete with these origin stories, and when the Lakota/Dakota Oyate say that "we were once the star people," they mean it literally because they understand the functions of storytelling as chronologies of the past and the future. There is probably no need to either lament or worship how these matters find their ways into contemporary literatures, though most of us react on one side or the other of it. The truth is, our literatures have suffered the oppression of colonial intrusion, much knowledge is forgotten or ignored, and we as native people have often been confused or disillusioned as to what it all means in terms of contemporary lives. Part of what has been going on in this intrusion is what I call "the master narrative," that is, the white man's version of who we are as native peoples. This master narrative is everywhere and it is blatant and it is in my view, at least, an arrogance that is unremitting. I live twenty miles from where the white man is blowing up a mountain to sculpt the face of the great Oglala Chieftain Crazy Horse. We all know that Crazy Horse DID NOT ALLOW his photograph to be taken. Thus, we Indians don't know what he looks like. But the white man does, and carves his face on a mountain he knew as sacred. How offensive is that arrogance? How important is it to the white man in America that the master narrative be supreme? How absurd!

The recent re-creation of the Lewis and Clark Journal, as a literary and historical manifestation of the American epic to be honored in our collective memories, is another example of that intrusion. It is told and retold not as a colonial event resulting in the death of thousands of Indians and the theft of a continent from peoples who had lived here for thousands of years; rather, it is told as an event of grand achievement. Much of what American Indian literary works have been doing has been to dispute that legacy of colonial intrusion and in doing so, mythic sensibilities are rediscovered and reclaimed. The master narrative is coming under closer scrutiny, and the return to tradition is becoming more important in the Native American Story.

The function of mythology, then, from which all ideas about origins emerge, is an essential part of that scrutiny. Lewis and Clark are newcomers to the stage, and they say almost nothing about the indigenous life of this continent. It is left up to the native to do that, and so concepts of indigenousness are developed, personalities are identified, events that shape eras are reviewed, geographies become the center of cultural endeavor. What I mean by that can be thought of in this way: Tate, the wind, is thought of as the "first Dakotah," and is called sometimes Ikce. Or even Ikca Wicasta. When the earth was covered only with water, he existed. He is considered a relative and an ancestor of the Dakotahs. He is male, like the Sun, and is sometimes thought to be a "bad" relative or a "good" one. He is a determinant, sometimes, of behavior. He is one of the ancestral spirits in native experience, one of the first characters in the stories to whom the question "What makes people behave as they do?" must be asked. This means that ethics and morality exist in the universe and it is up to human beings to pay attention.

When the Dakotahs and Lakotahs say, "We were once the star people," they, like the grandmother of the *Mahpiyato* story that first began this essay, pay homage to the Creators. When the wind was the only presence, and when the earth was covered with water, the stars were made from water, and they were us, Dakotahs. Thus, Dakotas know constellations as symbols of information formed to tell us what we need to know in order to live harmoniously on this earth. For example, there is a wonderful story about a particular constellation, called by non-Dakotahs the Big Dipper. You all know Big Dipper stories, I'm sure. Dakotas do, too. They call this star formation *wic'a ak'i'uhan pi*, which can be translated as "man being carried in the sky," and it is a reference to those seven stars that make up the constellation of the seven council fires of the Sioux Nation. Reference is made, then, to what we know here on earth . . . we are seven large bands: Oglala, Sicangu, Ihanktowan, Isianti, Minneconjou, Si Hasapa, and Hunkpati. You see, what is in the stars is on the earth and what is on the earth is in the stars. I refer to this constellation in my stories, once in *The Power of Horses* and again, I think, in my latest collection of essays, *Anti-Indianism in Modern America: A Voice from Tatekeya's Earth* (University of Illinois Press, 2001), as a way to explain the Dakotah way of life.

This is how I explain it:

Wic'a ak'i'uhan pi is a constellation that has four stars situated at the four points of what the non-Siouan world knows as the Big Dipper, along with three stars which make up the handle, seven stars in all. These four plus three points in the constellation are thought to be "carriers," defined with sacred status. They are carriers of the seven sacred rituals of the people, and therefore are repositors of religious knowledge. Further, they are considered to be four spirit people (or six or seven) who often assist other humans,

12

sometimes carrying them, in the journeys across the skies during the ohunkaka (creation) period, toward humanity.

This myth is often re-created in the rituals of the people even today. For example, I continue to explain:

This act of assistance is often recreated in a modern Lakota/Dakota/Nakota dance ritual known in English as "the blanket dance," when four dancers (usually male traditional dancers, though sometimes in recent more modern decades, young women dancers) hold the four corners of a blanket and make a journey around the dance arena asking that donations be placed in the blanket for the singers who, it is always said, "have come from a far distance" and need assistance on their homeward journey. The truth is, they probably just came from around the corner, up the street, or a few miles away, yet the mythic notion of assistance throughout the universe is a truth replayed over and again. You can see this played out at any Sioux pow-wow, if you are inclined to go to these summer gatherings. So, the point is ancient mythic knowledge, fragile as it is, persists in our everyday lives.

The miracle is that any of this has survived. But one of the reasons to continue to tell the stories is to remind all of us that we are in danger of losing respect for all living things, including each other. We have lost some kind of communal common sense and we really do need to talk to one another about how to bring about a new period in our concomitant histories.

It is important to know that the business of history and myth and identity for American Indians and for all of us is a complex matter. It deserves our attention. Yet the sober truth is that the white man's burden of winning the West and taking over this continent, which, by the way, is the subject of much of my political writings, has dealt a crushing blow to all of this worldview that I have been describing here briefly. The Americans' history, in my view, what is called the manifest destiny colonization of this continent, is one of the crimes of human history. And, now, it would seem that America will move on from this dark and bloody ground, to the winning of the entire globe, if what is going on in the Middle East is any measure. The deaths of thousands of Iraqis and the destruction of their cities and their civilization, their art and geography, seem to be inconsequential. Modern Americans have become the Spanish Conquistadors who burned to the ground the temples of the Incas, the Mayas, and the Aztecs, as well as the northern tribes. I would venture to say the indigenous peoples of this continent are not surprised at this recent turn of events.

In spite of the crimes of history, we write. We continue as artists, poets, novelists, fictionists, parents, grandparents. We continue to want the stories. We have little power, but that does not mean we have no influence. I have come to the conclusion that it is not my overriding business to create new ways of looking at the world in order to come up with smart and effective solutions for every case. It is my business to remember ... to remember the past and recall the old ways of the people. Literature and art, myth and history have always been the way to shape a new world.

I want to remind my readers again, as I often do, about one of the first things I published after I started my professional career. It was in a little chapbook called *Then Badger Said This*, now out of print. It is about remembering the past. It is about a tattoo (one of the important ways of writing for the Sioux in the old days). It is about the Badger and it is about storytellers, and it is about grandmothers. But, mostly, it's about art and mythology and the human condition. It really tells you something about tribal writers, I think. It tells you that for me, as a writer, I see everything in the world through the prism of my tribal experiences. I see everything in the world through the prism of the theft of the sacred Black Hills . . . which tried to make us accept our lives as beggars . . . out there on the Crow Creek. I see everything through the prism of native language and those who went ahead who did not write their names in English. Here is a brief paragraph that reflects all of that. The first time I heard this story, it was told to me by an elder relative and she told me that the Badger had said this, and so, years later, I wrote it down.

> *Keyapi.* (They say this.) When the Dakotapi really lived as they wished, they thought it important to possess a significant tattoo mark. This enabled them to identify themselves for the grandmothers who stood on the ghost road entering the spirit world asking: *takoja* . . . where is your tattoo? If the Dakotah could not show them his mark, they pushed that one down an abyss and he never reached the spirit land.

That doesn't sound too much, at first glance, like a grandmotherly thing to do, does it? On the contrary, it tells you, as all grandmothers do, to remember who you are! It says you must be able to identify yourself as a Dakotah for the grandmothers who are standing on the ghost road . . . yes? The tattoo is merely the outward symbol for that otherwise-profound identity.

Well, you know, the Badger said many things. He is always in Dakota stories and he is always asked many questions even though he is not important, not like Coyote or The Trickster, or Unktomi or Ikce or any of the others. But, he always has something to say ... he always has an answer .... Sometimes he is right but, just as often, he is wrong. Quite wrong.

But what he does, you see, is ... he keeps the plot moving .... Without him, you see, the story would come to an early and unsatisfactory end.

The Inadequacy of Literary Art

The art of writing poems is unlike
playing and listening to the sounds of the traditional Dakotah flute.
Once when I was talking to a Dakotah flute player and composer
and listening to him play, he said: *what I play on the flute with*
my fingers and my breath make the story I want to tell but I don't use words.
    He carefully held his wood flute to his lips,
       and the sounds,
like those large pony beads we use in decoration, fell around us.
They replaced the porcupine quills in some new unknown patterns,
no labels,
no boundaries inventing anew a liturgy that had
no interest in covering the ecumenical debate I've spent my life as a
writer, a user of words, trying to answer
that one-sided debate
about whether or not the Dakotah Sioux are still
to be known
as killers
of innocents.

This Story

I've just told you when I played the song,
     the flute player said
     when the long and excessive
     sounds echoed its unbearable memory
     neither of us could put into words, *it is very sad.*

It is about a woman who is leaving, and she turns and waves her shawl, and he thinks he may not see her again. But, I don't have to tell you that story in words, I can just tell it with the sounds of the flute. Words can be part of it, he said, *but they aren't necessary.*

What? What? Words aren't necessary?

This puzzling dilemma is a Dakotah theory of art that has its counterpart, one supposes, in all theories, even in non-Dakotah theory, as all writers struggle to know the meaning of words, the fundamentals of language.

This dilemma for writers of imaginative work, whose only tools are words, needs more theoretical examination, I suppose, but what it suggests is that musicians can disregard the usual elements of writing in English (or any other language), the ubiquitous plot, the tedious endings and beginnings, the flamboyant character and, for god's sake, the excruciating EXPOSITION.

The Woman Who Wrote Poems

She wrote 448 poems
all of them starting with the first-person "I"
like Karen Blixen who had only her coffee plantation
in a foreign country to embrace her; lovers leaving,
fires burning still, no one demonized for abandoning her:
she went back to England   alone   alone   no cures
for self-absorption   ever to feel nothing but the going.

What she learned from the isolation of writing
448 dreadful poems is hard to say . . .
unlike Welch who turned away
from the magic of Richard Hugo
toward writing novels,

she carried on the awful curse.

no eclipse
no coming back. Perhaps it's a handicap to be a writer of 448 poems
forever locked in time. Perhaps not . . . if what you crave is
a great battering and slashing.

In This

the winter of my writing life
I see the handwriting on the wall.

paint peeling on the window sill
crippled trees shadowing
the sun flooding the room

I see a daunting landscape of wild fate, my own vanity
mirrored flat and shabby and indistinct

time now to rephrase, repaint, repair

I don't know you well enough to let you choose
the wallpaper or keep paint cans from tipping;
yet, I'll take your hand, scorn my fears,
and move with you toward rooms,
hallways, maybe even the stairs.

No last stand as exotic as the interior scenes I've drawn,
just the last of the red geraniums on the steps,
unused words I wish I'd written on walls covered with crimson

and one last verse at the edge of falling snow.

There Is Something Off-Stage
(moments alone at writer's workshop)

Open pages of a manuscript flung on the hotel's table,
numbers by the phone flashing red, half-full boxes
of greasy Hunan noodles, things that
fend off the bearded editor's words: "leave here
thinking if you write something *really good*, it will
find an audience." Failing to broker a deal for a glib
novel, he wrote three memoirs and began
talking about them at one workshop too many.

Me, I'm alone in a room across the street from the
Cleveland Theatre where Toni Tennille plays a woman
playing a man playing a woman. Cast-off sapphires,
sparkle of neon, immaculate lights in the dark sky.
Some become the rejected stars writing book reviews and
memoirs, some play a woman playing a man long past starlight,
and others just keep the faith knowing that in the spring
we move to the creek we've always called That Place.

The grizzled editor, distributed now by Norton, tells us
he prepares to write yet another memoir. It will be clever.
Emotionally hollow. Ironic. Complicated. This recurring
sense of hope and despair interrupts artful compositions
which fail to catch leftover light between passions,
panhandling words, and pages of tribal histories
no one here even knows.

Written in Kindness and Gratitude for the White Women Who Are Peace and Justice Volunteers

You know what it's like standing
in flimsy wraps, shouting ad hoc political
manifestos on a windswept corner
where Dick's Donuts warms shadows
of a courthouse filled with third-rate
lawyers, bank presidents, overbearing
arbitragers leaning toward
windows, staring

you know what it's like to speak like historians
into the dogged vastness of a cow town's
brainless and cynical disinterest

you know smart Indians with white words
who cajole and urge and educate
in hopes of repatriation

but what you don't know is
what it means to be
daughters to those tribal men seeing
homelands only through dim jail cell
mirrors, men conjuring fascinated grandsons
who, if they read this, will be much older now

and their eyes will shine.

Books in Missoula

It's not my kind of bookstore
because Vine is absent
and McMurtry is under History

it's America's place for
screening what is peripheral
where the beginning of ideology
is theory and Gore Vidal's
mixed blessings
where the argument, fitting itself
into any middle-class mode of
intellectualism is about
insiders and outsiders

it's an Amish Market
a land of Country Inns where
Indian masks sell for a hundred dollars
and mists cover the land and
"trust Jesus" signs ask
how to change the world

On an August night, strolling
between the bookshelves
I hear faint strains of *love, true love
don't come knocking on my door*

and suddenly realize I'm lost
in a Threepenny Shop at 1600 Hardin Place

The pretenders are here
asking where they do mercy killings of Indians
who now and then appear from the wilderness
to walk the honky-tonks, barflies or great dancers

I don't want to sound pious
but I am a contemplative reader
of Derrida's theory
that says we cannot go
beyond the text.

Messages as I Pass a Car

overturned in the ditch
wheels still spinning
"God is my co-pilot"
reads the sign
in the rear window

as I drive
through damp little
towns toward Seattle
I look to the mountains
see clear-cut slashes
and read another sign:
"Isn't It Time for Jesus?"

at the motel
I read words of the white woman
about Lost Bird
in a compendious
examination
of the daily life and
year after year survival
of the suffragette
who adopted the Indian orphan
picked up from the massacre site
by the murdering soldier

later, lying on my back
in the sun I read
poems by
white nature boys,
describers of road kills

change is inevitable
yet some ideas are not all that new
Voltaire, I muse, was (mercifully) dead
before *Candide* became
a musical on Broadway
in New York. And Shakespeare,
too, who doesn't have to suffer
the sight of lovers running
through darkened streets,
carrying Uzis, hides out now in
the Devil's English called cinema

We are told by Monahan
on a radio interview
that the failure of tribal
nationalism is what
encourages Indians
in their ethnic thumb sucking
and Heaney says
the end of art is peace

"Horror and Moral Terror
are your friends," says the

Apocalypse Now character
played by Marlon Brando

helping us to the
realization that
we who are colonized
must cut off inoculated arms
that it is moral to utilize
the instinct to kill
with neither passion
nor judgment

it defeats us

we're told

by those who have
no stake in humanity

on behalf
of the first peoples
I say little about what
these messages mean
concerning the pursuits of life
by fellow human beings

like everybody else
I take the path
of least resistance.

Hearing Spiders Pray...

There is a wonderful poem about tourists in Indian Country that
appears in Jim Barnes's *A Season of Loss* and somehow it reminds me
of a real tenet: "the shattering of cultures is a terrible thing, yet history
stops for no one." The Polish writer Irena Klepfisz and a hundred
others who survived the Holocaust in Europe tell you as much! I like
the idea that history stops for no one because for American Indians,
the wind and the spiders that Barnes recalls in this long poem enfold
us even today, as we are immersed in the indigenous world of those
who have gone before. Barnes was talking of Santa Fe, New Mexico,
where he was giving a reading:

> Here the wind is a bad witch from the north:
> beans and tumbling stones, sheep and hogans,
> grip the earth when sand blasts adobe raw.
>
> Leaving Santa Fe is no mean task. You steel
> yourself against an afternoon of ease,
> feeling a new grip forced into your guts.
> the last pueblos know the wind better
> than any tourist.   (p. 22)

"You hear spiders pray," he goes on, "as the wind touches bells that
do not sound and doors to the cathedral forever locked against a night
that's bound to arrive on time." This poet's attempt to create what I call
a "cultural landscape" is inevitable in spite of the shattering of worlds
so obvious in the political and historical dialogue that takes place
over and over as we speak of the "Indian experience." The process by

28

which we do what Barnes has done in this poem is to combine a tribal experience, a tribal mythic history, and a tribal imagination. This isn't my theory of a cultural landscape. It, perhaps, belongs to no one. But, the first I heard of it was when I listened to N. Scott Momaday talk of his work decades ago.

Imagination is the key word here. I honor the idea that the Sioux dare to imagine who they are in connection with a specific place. For thousands of years the Dakotas (the Sioux) have done this, and so have the Choctaws and the Pueblos of this poem.

People who read my work

know that I am still angry that the DeFunis and Bakke cases have been interpreted by most people as ARGUMENTS FOR PRIVILEGED ADMISSION rather than arguments against the positive and historical benefits received by the privileged class (that is, the mainstream or the majority or the wealthy) in this country. Still angry, though I have a daughter (one of a precious few) who has managed to enter the legal profession and now works for justice in Indian country. I am still angered when I hear the continued attacks upon the federally mandated "affirmative action" strategies that allowed people like myself to enter the humanities centers of this country decades ago. I am angry that because of the "backlash," it has become more and more difficult at the turn of the twenty-first century for young Indian people of scant means to get there. Recent statistics tell us that fewer and fewer Indians are entering these Ivy halls, as these attacks continue. It is often asked, is there any reason why university training, let alone jurisprudence and medicine as professions should be held in protective custody by the caste system of mainstreamness and majorityness? Have the legal systems benefited from this? Have scholarship and research benefited? Do we have better medical treatment in this country because of this privilege?

Surrounded by Serbs on Rapid Creek

(lines written at a meeting in the Black Hills of
museum curators)

They're all the same, these immigrant children
of exiles from ruined Europa, Europa
here in America disguised as bankers, secretaries
and clerks, lawyers and teachers
white people with forgotten histories, desperate for legacy
diplomats for kleptocracies, learning to close doors softly

seeing them here I recognize the contempt
they have for themselves and others

prospering still on Indian lands
the semite architect from Malibu
his heart in the right place
smiles and rubs his knuckles in the cold
talks of invasion as encounter
genocide as convergence

having escaped their own murder by relatives
in ruined Bosnia, Czech land, Europa,
Europa, the grievous centuries of blooded hatred,
they are here to make us understand
the nature of their boldly pursued civility:
impoverish the Sioux, dissolve by

congressional fiat the Alaskan natives,
run down the Nez Perce and starve the Hopi
occupy the land, occupy the land,
tell the smiling stories
of encounter and convergence

adventurers, painters of Indian chiefs
who settle beyond the *miniluzaha*
and describe McGillycuddy as heroic
are here again with funded money,
just like the guitar player said,
to tell their stories.

Birds, Yellow Jackets, the Sun, and an Old Man

they land in the grass and the greasewood
to feast on whatever seeds cover the ground
they hide in the hillside, silent for long moments
then swoop into the sky again
hundreds of them
bursting away in the dead heat

they hang in the eaves of the log house
dizzy in the hot sun
hanging
touching
slipping into my glass
of sweet wine
drawn there
by the tint
or the fragrance
or the syrup

it puts shadows
at the side of every autumn bush
like the agent of creation
whose inevitability
drips from pale hands of time

he eats a grapefruit
spears chunks with a

slender, well-handled knife
then turns back to a book
about sailboats
and jibs
and wind currents

the afternoon sun wanes and
shadows deepen
I can't tell
what is ending

II

In shaping a poem, it is interesting to play sentences off against lines. But to write a poem that is one long sentence requires that you be particularly creative. Use coordinating conjunctions, elaborate, modify and expand. You improve your prose writing through this practice in poetry because you discipline yourself, usually, to delay the point. The longer the sentence, the longer the delay. The following three poems, "Who Owns the Past?" "Thoughts While Driving across a Bridge on Interstate 90," and "A Younger Sister, I Try to Believe in Myself," are examples of sentence poems.

Who Owns the Past?

When people like Henry Louis Gates
ask this question out of hearing distance, naturally, of
college Western Civ classes, they turn the conversation
to America, understanding Africa in the Black Vernacular Tradition,
getting lost in the dialogue of Alice Walker's Celie and Shug,
forgetting about "Naipaul's Fallacy" and agreeing with
almost everything that's said about how wrong the
Modern Language Association is concerning The Trickster Figure
in Chicano/a and Native and Black Literatures said to make
Borderlands just a matter of Semantics.

Thoughts While Driving across a Bridge on Interstate 90

What's the point of the water monster plaguing
Indians, racking them with pain and fever and death
because when things go bad the Ikce know they have been
given herbs and roots and the people will be saved by
steam and smoke and what's the point of fearing Death
if you know Shunk and Pahin have carried
the alienated one out of this world to be by himself
after he taught them about hot stones and how to
wear the red stripe where hair is parted in the middle
and what's the point of fearing Death when you
know, anyway, that he is also, with red hair all over,
breaking up the ice on the river in spring.

A Younger Sister, I Try to Believe in Myself

Now I am remembering how I buried my mother alone
without the angry, unforgiving sibling who, ordinarily tolerant
but with uncontrollable defensiveness persists in the overt
denial that unintentional maternal weaknesses, like inevitable registered
letters, cling to memory and rituals, delivered and loved and distorted
so that even the most sincere and dutiful convictions of polite refusal
can't be reported as anything new, can't go without saying prayers,
can't be inherited and only now, with greater maturity, can I be
truthful and say that when I tried to dissuade her from her refusal I
didn't try hard enough and didn't really want to because it is possible, as
I've already mentioned, to be persuaded by a daughter's arguments
        concerning
the stinging of unintentional maternal weaknesses.

Another Place to Walk Back From
(an excerpt from the novella *Roads*)

I know my country well.
And I know its duplicity.

Nobody needs to tell me what it means
that my eldest uncle disappeared after the 1973 uprising

and we never saw him again and the federal police
kept asking for him and I went along thinking he might be

just another mythic figure like Tonto or Luke Skywalker

Nobody needs to tell me that all crimes on the Indian Reservations
of this country no matter how trivial become felonious and that a

lethal combination of booze and drugs causes the death
of guys I know walking out of Nebraska toward home
Nobody needs to tell me it's a long walk.

This is the place where those kinds of lives are notorious
but a place, too, where just hours away there are expensive hospitals

and white doctors a few hundred miles from the places I know so poor
Indian women with children at the knee simply walk down to the water

and never come back, humiliated by the abandonment
of desperate men, insulted by the old hypocritical ways of the nuns

Or where Indians suffering from mental deficiencies are just stuffed
in garbage cans and left to choke to death on their own saliva.

In the expensive shiny hospital where I worked when I was
young, the doctors were so bored with life and death and luxury and

terrible food they just didn't care anymore. It's paradoxical to say
this was the place where I learned what drugs could do

Not from the streets of border towns or Indian Reservation dumps.
Not from the frenzied white-mouthed druggies of downtown or
behind

taverns. I learned it here in a white woman's private room with
drawn drapes and artificial crab-apple blossoms brought by the

husband every day and placed with geraniums in a bowl of water.

The white woman, like so many others from around here
was rich, well known in the upscale community of this college town.

She weighed now less than ninety pounds and was said by her friends
to be suffering from "exhaustion." She had been here with her

lawyer husband in attendance years before I got here, yet she would
be in my memory long after I left. Not because she was so unique

but because she wasn't.

☙

Who Are You, Tim McVeigh?
June, 1986

I wonder if I know you
the self-crowned son
of White America: a soldier, a brother

the time is past and today is tomorrow
and tomorrow is yesterday and today
is a time you come face to face
with America, assuming since birth
the reach of the law is for others

America's emergence from
myth and the geography of hope
has helped you crown yourself

with good conscience

America is unambiguous
not changeable like the
falling autumn leaves
from invisible trees along the
knowable rivers

there is no forest
no stillness, no branches

             but on a
wooden bier for native grief
is Sitting Bull's coffin
at the Grand River,
the mark of self-crowned
conscience is
hidden by the shadow
of yesterday's militia
to be born on the exploding wind
of today at the right moment

your last gestures
of the self-crowned
are tomorrow's history
        and today's yesterday

there is no way out of the
self love of a patriot son
who wants to do heroic deeds

                                              1986

III ∂∂∂

June

2004

Eulogy to Ronald Reagan

Your stage voice speaks of a city on a hill
a new Jerusalem, the English Reformation
and capitalism: land, commodities, labor
all up for grabs in a world that glorifies
war and conquest, conversion and rehab.
Remember when you said as an American, "we have
indulged those Indians far too long," a political
notion for all those who watched the next
John Wayne movie.

Biblical scenes of battle and "Onward Christian Soldiers"
stories are the cultural ancestry for all Americans, you
said. Given the proper conditions, and for the moment,
they'll all believe you: one false move and you'll draw your six guns.

Aurelia: A Crow Creek Trilogy

Novella by Elizabeth Cook-Lynn

About This Guide

This guide is meant to give insight into the unique aspects of a book (*Aurelia: A Crow Creek Trilogy*) which has been described by the many editors who have read it as outside of the cultural mainstream of American fiction and has as its essential interest the examination of a particular indigenous and historical lifeway and experience.

Writer Victor Hernandez Cruz says that this book shows the reader "the intersection where mythology, history, religion and politics meets within a strong storytelling tradition." These are clues to exposition of the novel.

The story is set in real time, between 1950 and 1990, and in a real place, the indigenous homelands of the Dakota Crow Creek Sioux Indians of South Dakota, an Indian Reservation of some 300,000 acres situated along the Missouri River about 50 miles from the capital city of SD, Pierre. Protagonists John Tatekeya and Aurelia Blue are the main characters along with the Big Pipe Family and other tribal members who are culturally Isianti (Santee) and Ihanktowan (Yankton) Dakota Sioux Indians.

Historical Background

The Santee Indians signed early treaties with the United States (1851), fought the Little Crow War (1862) because of treaty violations, and were placed on the Crow Creek Reservation in 1863. They were dispersed, also, at Flandreau, Sisseton, Niobrara, Nebraska; many ended up in Canada and on meager homelands in Minnesota. They were close allies with the Yankton Indians, and a part of the Sioux Ocheti: Oglala, Hunkpati, Minneconjou, Sicangu, and Si Hasapa.

In 1868 the Fort Laramie Treaty was ratified by Congress to establish peace between the United States and the Sioux Tribes which comprise the Sioux Nation. It established a 26 million acre reserve (The Great Sioux Reservation) for the "absolute and undisturbed use and occupation" of the Sioux Oyate. The diminishment of these reserved lands and the structures of tribal poverty developed by law and occupation and congressional and executive order has been the history of the last one hundred years for Sioux Indians in the Northern Plains.

In 1924 and 1934 citizenship was conferred by the United States upon Sioux Indians and "token" governments set up through "reorganization" legislation. America's brand of Democracy had come to Indian Country.

In 1950 Attorney Ralph Case filed the Sioux (Lakota/Nakota/Dakota) tribes' original petition in the Indian Claims Commission on August 15. The case was docketed as "Docket 74." The Cheyenne River Sioux Tribe, Crow Creek Sioux Tribe, Lower Brule Sioux Tribe, Oglala Sioux Tribe, Rosebud Sioux Tribe, Santee Sioux tribe of Nebraska, Sioux Tribe of Fort Peck Reservation, Standing Rock Sioux tribe were parties to Docket 74.

In 1980, having proven to the courts that their lands were taken "illegally," the Docket 74 Sioux were awarded $102 million for Black Hills land and $3 million for placer gold and three rights-of-way, but no return of lands. Much tedious litigation ensued. The tribes today remain steadfast in rejection of what is now called Docket 74-A and 74-B awards, demanding instead the restoration of title to federal lands in both claims areas. Lawyers for the United States and the courts say that the case is settled. The Sioux do not agree.

This land issue, the contemporary Sioux say, is inseparable from the forty-year United States military war and peace strategy which resulted in various acts of genocide, that is, the largest hanging in the history of the United States of 38 Santee Dakota Indians in Mankato, Minnesota, in 1862 and the killing of nearly 400 unarmed Minneconjou Lakotas at Wounded Knee less than eighteen years later, to name just two. It is also inseparable from a vicious colonial history which has resulted in a political relationship between the Sioux and the United States underlying a "title by conquest" situation which is maintained by colonial manipulation and the result is, they say, no justice even today. The question: *How can a native people survive within and alongside their historical oppressors?* is not a rhetorical question. It describes the daily dilemma which confronts Indians everywhere on this continent but, particularly in the Northern Plains, the setting for *Aurelia: A Crow Creek Trilogy.*

The story opens (in the *From The River's Edge* section) with a cattle theft trial which has taken place during the flooding of thousands of acres of treaty protected Indian land along the Missouri River for the purpose of developing hydro power in the Northern Plains. This act of developing hydro power which is considered contemporary "progress" was initiated by the United States Government (the tribal "trustee") without tribal-nation sanction or approval in contradiction to known protective laws against it.

A personal and individual trial on behalf of a Sioux Indian landowner provides the essential plot device for the first section but, as the second story (*Circle of Dancers*) and the third and final narrative (*In The Presence of River Gods*) unfolds it is clear that the building of the dams and the destruction of the Missouri River lands of the tribal people who occupy them serves as a metaphor about a myriad of crimes perpetuated by a colonial United States government against a sovereign tribal people. The trial (from which there are no winners) is thought by some to be ultimately irrelevant except as an organizational device to tell readers that this is the first of many crimes committed against indigenous peoples in the Northern Plains during the twentieth century.

When we first see the plaintiff, John Tatekeya, he is sixty years old, married with children and grandchildren, beginning what will be a ten-year love affair with Aurelia Blue, who is thirty years younger than he and trying to survive the upheaval brought about by the flooding of the tribal homelands. In the final pages of the third story Tatekeya is blind, unable to walk, still the Santee Sioux spokesperson who believes that it is important to expose the devastating consequences of federal officials "practicing deceit" upon Native American Tribes. Aurelia Blue, witness to decades of tribal history, leaves Tatekeya after nearly ten years to become a wife and mother. She bears a son (the essential act of the Corn Wife of Dakota mythology) for Jason Big Pipe and is known among the people as one who possesses the tribal story.

Aurelia can be said to be a story a tribal family in the twentieth century and it is about loss. It can also be said to be a story about injustice. But, mostly, it is a story about crime, both the institutional crime of theft of tribal lands and individual crimes like murder and rape. It is a story which encompasses particular crimes none of which result in just verdicts. The Tatekeya trial concerning stolen cattle in 1968 in the first novella suggests that theft on an Indian Reservation is not punished, and the trial concerning a rape in 1995 the final story suggests that hate crimes have neither punishment nor public hearing. Crime, mainstream America is often told, requires a response, that is, investigation, public hearing, punishment. The exception to this rule plays out in Indian Country where the prosecution of crimes is inadequate or delayed, and results only in betrayal and deprivation. Perhaps *Aurelia*, the novel, is the response to the crimes talked of here.

For Discussion

1. Probably one of the essential questions of this novel is: How is present crime related to historical crime? Or, is it?

2. Much of the beginning story in *Aurelia* is dependent upon *irony*. Explain the use of *irony* in the story-within-a-story technique (p. 38–39) and what is its connection to the trial? to the development of the protagonist John Tatekeya? to the contrast between storytelling and contemporary fiction writing?

3. What are the Dakota mythologies concerning the river and women that are essential to this story? What are some other mythic figures important to the thematic structure of the novel?

4. How does nature shape this novel?

5. Aurelia's youthful decision to become Tatekeya's lover is essential to defining her role as a Dakotah Wiyan (Sioux Woman). Explain.

6. If intermarriage is seen by many in America as a way to "integrate" in a culturally diverse society, what are the thoughts on that notion expressed by the Indians in this Crow Creek society?

7. In many contemporary stories about Indians in America, as well as other so-called "minority" characters, there is usually a huge struggle about identity issues. In *Aurelia*, there is very little

acknowledgment of "doubleness," or what has been described as personal identity conflict between being Indian and being American revealed in these fictional characters. They rarely express the idea that they are Native Americans. Yet, they are rooted to this place called America, and are, more than most, subject to American law, American governmental practice. What does this suggest about cultural conflict in a so-called "diverse" society? What are the notions concerning reconciliation between races that can be offered in the telling of this story? Does this distinguish the American Indian experience from, for example, the experience of African Americans or Asian Americans. If so, how so?

8. The 1988 "Epilogue," p. 340, expresses the *tragedy* of Sheridan Big Pipe. It is expressed almost as a penultimate narrative, something like the "lost letter" approach Herman Melville used in the novella called "Bartleby." What does the author accomplish in using this technique? One clue to discussing this is to note that this information is given outside of the actual plot of the story. Using a literary definition of "tragedy," explore what this means in tribal terms and in connection with tribal values?

9. Do some research on the female mythic figure called Corn Wife, or Yellow Woman and discuss Aurelia's role as a contemporary Indian woman in the context of mythology.

10. Many flashbacks are used in the telling of these three stories. What is the function of memory as it concerns conscience and morality and personal behavior? Give specific examples.

The Old Couple

To visit them
I drive over prairie hills
past the sea of green all round
where the horizon meets the vast
washed blue of the sky opening up
for the day. I circle toward the agency
and the land dips into draws
thick with cottonwoods.

The sun burns white
and my fingers grip the steering wheel
not yet ready to comb her hair and ransack
the drawers for matches to light his smokes.
The anticipation of venerable days they will tell me about
soothes the racket of bald tires hitting gravel and gumbo.
I see faded wrinkles in my grip, age lines, dark spots and veins
looking like her hands as they will fold and unfold in her lap.

The sun flashes on dried yarrow and wild onions
along the road and my eyes stare behind the waves
to ancient moorings leaving no route for forgetting.
When I get there I will do the meanest chores, smiling.
Together, the old couple constantly dazzles the light with
flower-soft hands and reminds me that age cannot wither them.

Another Commencement Address
(from a hotel on Wilshire Boulevard)

If I could remember the floods, the hurricanes,
plagues, wars, the ceremonies and deliveries
that brought me here, I would ask what they mean
to youthful discoverers, Xers, museum keepers
and outlaws, urgency your new and only direction:

hey, what can you say to someone born in 1980?

Luminous as the night image of Getty's collections sparkling
over my left shoulder, those hopes and dreams of yours cannot
be seen in dim past light, yet here in this café on the 17th floor
on your first anniversary as masters I realize you yearn
soberly for the world that came before. Hanay knows that,
too, so he invites speakers and panelists to illuminate the old
stories in the newest sunlight, tells me
he will go back to Oklahoma
when he is an old man

then he will remember the floods, the hurricanes,
the plagues, wars and ceremonies.

In the meantime, enduring mysteries of who we are and
who we can become we willfully and wantonly
pursue such moments of grace as we try desperately
to emerge from the luminous present

toward insignificant and forgotten days.

What I Really Said at the UCLA Indian Studies Commencement 2004

It is my pleasure to be here. *Mitakuyapi, owasin cantewasteya nape ciyuzapi do!* (My relatives, with a good heart I greet all of you with a handshake.) Thank you for the invitation.

There are so many thing to say on an occasion like this. And, lately, I've felt that I have to apologize since I think that as a writer . . . since I've been writing all those snotty little essays . . . I think I am getting the reputation of being a slash-and-burn kind of critic. I have had nothing good to say about politicians, anthropologists, white people who muck around in Indian Country. So, I've gotten this bad reputation as a mean-spirited writer of bad reviews. Nothing, of course, could be further from the truth. . . . I'm terribly sweet natured and easy to get along with. I wrote *Why I Can't Read Wallace Stegner* and all the historians came out of the woodwork and invited me to all of their conferences . . . to argue with me about what I was calling the corrupt western myth. The book really wasn't about Stegner . . . just one essay was about his work. Then, my next collection is called *Anti-Indianism in Modern America* and all kinds of people don't speak to me any more . . . even some people I considered my friends. (My next book is called *New Indians and Old Wars* and I can expect more of the same.) But, thanks for the invitation to be here. . . . I'm very pleased.

This is about you, you see, not me. . . . This occasion of your completion of your studies. . . . Yes. . . . You are now at the beginning of your careers and it has been a difficult, challenging period for all of you. It is a hopeful, forward looking, intense, wonderful time in many ways, I think, very much like the time when I began my career decades ago, yet in many ways very different. It is worth discussing the differences that thirty years have made because the history of Indian Studies, which began in the 1970s, is a fascinating and marvelous period. Besides, on occasions like this, commencement speakers always like to tell you where they've been. . . .

Thirty years ago I had the opportunity and the privilege to start an academic career. I was teaching high school English and trying to keep a marriage together, both futile endeavors . . . . My career has been, I think, in answer to the call of Affirmative Action though I didn't know much about that then. Affirmative Action, as we all know now, was and is a national effort to move American Indians into Academic life . . . to become something more than mere "informants for curious anthropologists," or vulnerable subjects for largely unethical social science investigations. Or graduates of trade schools and nursing institutions. We were to become professors, researchers, writers, thinkers. This has proven to be the best of times and the worst of times as Charles Dickens would have said; the best of times because it allowed many of us to develop our intellectual selves, which we would never have been able to do under ordinary circumstances, and, the worst of times because, unfortunately, Affirmative Action was to become a bad word in the academic vocabulary (even for a lot of the people who benefited from it), as the right wing, conservative Americanists among us rose to power. The truth is, I'm bitter about the backlash we all suffered.

This is what I said when I wrote my first collection of those snotty little essays I mentioned, called *Why I Can't Read Wallace Stegner*, in 1996:

It (this remarkable time) was a conversion experience for everyone concerned. Only much later following the backlash to affirmative action articulated successfully in such litigation as the Bakke Case, the subsequent writings of several "minority" scholars such as Shelby Steele and Richard Rodriguez, and the flawed thinking which emerged during the Reagan presidency, was affirmative action dismissed as a noble idea. For my part, the affirmative action years gave me a brief vision of grace, the hope of a transcendent time when people like myself would be welcomed as American Indians into America's modern debates concerning society and knowledge which raged then and continue to rage today.

We were given many opportunities . . . . Nonetheless, in spite of the many opportunities I've had, I have to tell you that I have had a very inferior education. I was not chosen to go to Dartmouth or Harvard, UCLA, or even Yale where, apparently, C students can thrive on their way to the American presidency. I was not invited to sit on influential boards where great decisions were made. And the truth is, most of us had no great illusions even at the time that new doors were being opened. We knew that newspapers, the media, and social scientists still called us drunken Indians; that textbooks and movies still called us squaws and savages, and that legislators were still stealing the land.

Yet, it has been my privilege to have joined those Indian scholars who emerged in the 1970s to develop American Indian Studies as an academic discipline. Many of those scholars have gone on to achieve great things. Deloria, Momaday, Wilkins, Gieogomah, Riding In, White Hat, Medicine, Warrior, Holm, Mihesuah, Bordeaux, Harjo, Fixico, Jojola, Ortiz, Sekaquaptewa, dozens more. We have charted careers in Indian Studies to do several things: to defend our indigenous legacies, that is, tribal legacies in the appropriate ways, to regulate academic studies about us; and to transform our present condition. I would not

58

be in academia at all if not for that opportunity afforded by affirmative action and I am grateful for those auspicious, passionate, risky, inflammatory and wondrous times. They changed my life.

It was not all uphill, though, and I wrote a strange little poem about it called "My Previous Life."

When I was thirty, my slim bone and muscle
stretching long and nervous like rolls of tissue paper wrapping
hot coals or bloody wounds, I stood in line at the bus stop with
my *chunskay*, hands caressing his old fishing pole, and my
beautiful daughters, a congregation of wide-eyed souls who trusted
then as now my extemporaneous sermons. We waited to be borne
southward to desert cities where we saw streets flooded with the
annual rainfall in ten-minute lightning bolts. That year was not the
beginning of our exquisite bond but its memory stretches like deer
    hide
on a drum, to make a sacred resound. In the night our luggage got
    off
in Denver and we beamed on through the darkness stripped of
toothbrushes and extra underwear vulnerable as naked
roses in the fall. In less time than it takes to tell of the fear and pain
of a vision dying, no secret so alive as that of a family unable to
complete itself, we U-Hauled it back to Crow Creek where we stood
in chilly mists like trees yellowed and spent, or old folks
at the care center singing tired songs of the past. Out
of the wind and safe. We were home again where silences
toward failed women of bad marriages imprison the future
of their children. We lighted candles in a church that didn't
want us and I took a job giving English assignments to

battered men who claimed they couldn't write worth shit,
fists swollen and at the ready. Eventually, we drove our
aging Pontiac to a college town which led us through days
designed by racist professors and disciplines that deserved to
be blown up, splintered and charred. In that place, still warm
from regular paychecks and full tables we grew to know that those
who suffer loneliness don't always learn to despise themselves
if their bellies are full.
I look back on that thirtieth year as a year of departure,
Everything before that, the trappings of a previous life
Of false hope, everything after, an acknowledgment
That nothing matters except the love
Of those who love you.

(from *I Remember the Fallen Trees,* pp. 47–48)

That expresses the beginning of my academic career. I am not going to
say here that there is nothing more satisfying than a long career like
mine in which I eventually become a respected professor and writer.
Because, in saying that, there is the assumption that we have made
steady progress as a country, as its landlords and citizens of the First
Nations, as a generation of parents and grandparents who teach the
children, when in fact, disturbing realities still face us: title to the
sacred Black Hills is still in enemy hands, the United States does not
disavow the criminal and devastating claim to "plenary power" over us
and our resources, the legal systems which make up Federal Indian Law
principles are racist, land is stolen by the states as we speak, and it's
still true that my tall good-looking Sioux grandsons are still the first
to be arrested on trumped charges by the police in any city in South
Dakota where we live. A sad postscript to this dismal history is that

it is still true that there is not much of a track record in America that tells us this great democracy wants to uphold Indian Treaty Rights and acknowledge Tribal Sovereignty and work with us toward developing efficient governing systems. Indeed, the cause of native peoples today ... indigenous peoples everywhere in the world ... is widely considered "lost" to assimilation and genocide and aggressive capitalism.

Recently, in the defense of Indian Tribal Governments, which some may argue is either the seat of sovereignty or entrenched colonialism, former Cherokee Chief Wilma Mankiller, one of the important spokespersons of my generation, recently made the observation that it is not only academia and the courts and in government from which threats to Indian Sovereignty are launched. She says public perception, in general and pervasive ways, engendered by the media, is now in the forefront of putting out misleading negative attacks against us and our governments. She says that the media attacks on us have gotten worse, especially since gaming tribes look as though they might have some success in economic development on Indian homelands that have been pockets of poverty for a hundred years! Heaven forbid that Indian Nations should share in the wealth of their own country.

Now, I know that many of you have been thinking about these matters and hope to make a difference once you get out there in the real world. But, since it is the custom for graduation speakers to draw on their own experiences, I want to try to say this evening about what it all has meant to me.... *as one who has taken up the writing profession.* A profession, of course, which I hope many of you will join. I feel guilty encouraging you, but like they say ... somebody's got to do it. I've made the observation before (usually in the privacy of my own thoughts) that there is nothing quite so uncalled for in this world as a writer. Unless, of course, you are Sherman Alexie or various movie makers, writing and making movies for fifteen-year-olds. Poets are something else. But, really, there is nothing so unappreciated as a thoughtful and reasonably intelligent writer, nothing so unnecessary and unremunerative . . . that means that no one makes any money writing (except those movie makers, certainly not poets). This has been true for all writers, not just Indian writers. . . . Take Hawthorne, as an example. Nobody knew what he was writing about. Or Melville . . . he had absolutely no audience during his entire lifetime. Or take Franz Kafka, not the best example, perhaps, but an electrifying one. . . . Writing about a man who turns into a bug? Remember *Metamorphosis*? Why write about a man turning into a bug, when you could just as well be out playing golf, or drinking a beer, or watching *The Sopranos* on television, or getting a face lift? Or, maybe, making a movie. Why, then? Why write?

There may be no real good answer to that. I want to say that I think I started writing because I liked language. I grew up in a home where two languages were spoken all the time . . . everybody talked Indian in those days and almost everybody talked English. . . . Then I went to a boarding school briefly to be sure . . . where we learned Latin. The Latin Mass in the Catholic Church. Later I went to an Episcopal girls' school where they taught Latin as one of the classical languages. I found that thinking about language was interesting. Truth is, I grew up with a lot of people who didn't use English well . . . and, of course, used Latin not at all. . . . But they were eloquent in Dakotah. And they were great talkers!!!

But, about writing, the truth is, as a writer today, I've found that few seem to care about the work that we do, the work itself. The other day someone asked me what my children and my family thought about my writing. I said, well, they aren't much interested. They have busy lives of their own, you know. In fact, they are quite often bored or even impatient when I try to talk to them about what I'm doing as a writer. It's like bringing up the subject of herpes or something contagious, stuff they'd rather not think about.

Meanwhile, there is no appreciable audience out there in the mainstream, either. Even when a writer like myself is being interviewed by literary or newspaper types, there is no discussion about the work itself. In fact, quite often the interviewer hasn't a clue about what you have written. You get questions like: What was your childhood like? Did you go to boarding schools and did you suffer from racial discrimination? Say, what?????? Of course I went to boarding schools and of course there was racial discrimination. But, what I write about and what consumes me is the vague distaste I have for a democratic nation that exempts the people from whom it stole the land. I write about the politics of hallowed ground and I write about anti-Indianism as a concept much like anti-Semitism as well as other racist ideologies . . . rising out of religiosity, specifically Christianity. I write that Wallace Stegner was wrong to honor yet regret the corrupt western myth, and I write about the destruction of the Missouri River and 550 square miles of treaty-protected lands for hydro power. . . . I write about things people don't want to hear. I try to analyze and critique. And it has taken me a long time to learn how to use English well, and to write coherently. *That is what I think your charge is, as recent American Indian graduates*, to write well, to be coherent, and to change the dialogue that has defamed us.

As a writer and professor, I am more certain than ever before that writing is at the ethical core of the nation building that is occurring on our homelands these days. Writing is at the ethical core of what we hope to bring to the dialogue of this continent of the twenty-first century. The implication of my writing, most of which is political in nature, is that to be an American Indian today is to *be a responsible repository for the reformation that occurred in the seventies* (and of course, long before that).... That is not to say that we are prohibited from writing and publishing third-rate novels (none of which I'm going to mention here) and insulting poetry of self-hatred (which I've already mentioned in previous writings), because we are after all the originators of free speech. This is not to imply that we are prohibited from explicating theological issues and teaching the rest of the world how to "walk the red road" no matter how futile that is. (Wasn't it Sitting Bull who said that the white man will never understand our religious connection to our lands?) This is not to say, either, that writing about "me," "me," "me," and that "who I am and where I am going" stories often called ethnographic biographies shouldn't be out there. Boring. Boring. Boring. But, it is to say that until we master a critical and political voice, the public perception of who we are as indigenous peoples will continue to be dangerous to the health of all tribal nations, just as Mankiller has suggested.

What we need to understand as those who are Indian Studies scholars, is that we are the bearers of an alternative narrative of this country. We have signed treaties with the United States government and we are, therefore, not children of ethnic America, immigrants, slaves, colonists. Our beginnings are as the landlords of this continent and our monomyth is the Popol Vuh, not Adam and Eve and Christianity. Because we have not gone away, disappeared, vanished or become assimilated, as it has been hoped by Americans, and because we have resisted, people deliberately misunderstand us. Most Americans deliberately refuse to understand why we object to Chief Illini's outrageous burlesque at football games, why we rage at the celebrations of Columbus Day, why we don't want the famed Oglala Chieftain Crazy Horse (Tashunka Witko) to be pictured in an imagined pose on bottles of beer. More to the point, why we object to blowing up a mountain in the sacred Black Hills to carve an ugly and false face of that same chieftain, no matter whose "permission" you say you have.

The essential word is *deliberate*. Americans *deliberately misunderstand* us. That is because America's vision of itself is embedded in a history of imperialism known throughout the world (as the Iraqis are finding out), and it is America's intention to absorb and assimilate. When American Indians do not assimilate, and absorb and vanish, the innocence of the colonizer, the innocence of the immigrant, the innocence of the émigré is called into question. The innocence of teaching our children that Americans have the right to take over our land and resources and treat us as though we have no history begins to buckle and tilt. When the American Indian Movement in the 1970s marched on Washington, D.C., to protest a devastatingly cruel Indian policy that made beggars of us all, and when they cheered Malcolm X's "the chickens are coming home to roost" speech, global America was astonished and horrified. It is a story that America does not want to hear.

As ethnic America settles itself into democratic, legal enclaves, claims land and resources for itself, it suggests that all is well in America when, in fact, the ghosts of American imperialism that pervade all of Indian America must still be accounted for. That is the "why" of my writing. . . .

Indians have been in a constant fight to retain their sovereign rights to nationhood. Indians have lost in the twentieth century two-thirds of their treaty-protected lands. They are poorer than any segment of American society, so, what must be concluded? That white rightness has been successful and that anti-Indianism has won out? What else can we conclude? Law has produced white rightness. It has produced white innocence, it has produced the innocence of immigration, the innocence of colonization. It is unfortunate to have to admit that law and legislation as they now function do not defend *the right to be an Indian*. They do not defend the indigenous peoples of this world. Because I have spent a lot of time writing about the Black Hills land case, I have come to the conclusion that unless something is done concerning how law is written in this country concerning Indian land issues, we must conclude that Indian laws made by the colonizer are nonactionable. There is no action concerning theft and genocide toward native peoples. Writers can do little except point out these crimes of history. We have no power but that does not mean that we have no influence. I have come to the conclusion that it is not my overriding business to create new ways of looking at the world and come up with smart and effective solutions to every case. It is my business to remember . . . to remember the past and the old ways of the people. Literature and myth have a lot to do with a people remembering who they are and the function of writing both fiction and nonfiction, both poetry and storytelling, to shape that reality. . . .

You know in closing, and at the risk of sounding repetitious, I want to say something about one of the first things I published after I started my professional career. It was in a little chapbook called *Then Badger Said This*, now out of print. It is about remembering the past . . . it is about a tattoo (one of the important ways of writing for the Sioux in the old days), and it is about the Badger and it is about storytellers, and it is about grandmothers. . . . And it really tells you something about tribal writers. For me, as a writer, I see everything in this world through the prism of my tribal experiences. I see everything in the world through the prism of the theft of the Black Hills ... and our lives out on the Crow Creek.... I see everything in the world through the prism of our native language and those who went ahead. So, I will end with a story that reflects all of that.

The first time I heard this story, it was told to me by an elder relative and she told me that the Badger had said this and I wrote it down:

> *Keyapi.* (They say this.) When the Dakotapi really lived as they wished, they thought it important to possess a significant tattoo mark. This enabled them to identify themselves for the grandmothers who stood on the ghost road entering the spirit world asking: *takoja* ... where is your tattoo? If the Dakotah could not show them his mark, they pushed that one down an abyss and he never reached the spirit land.

Now, doesn't sound too much like a grandmotherly thing to do, does it? But, you know, the Badger said many things. He is always in Dakota stories and he is always asked many questions even though he is not important, not like Coyote, or The Trickster, or Unktomi or Ikce or any of the others. But, he always has something to say, he always has an answer. Sometimes he is right. Just as often, he is wrong. But, what he does is this ... *he keeps the plot moving. Without him, you see, the story would end.*

So, in closing ... it is my admonition ... to keep the plot moving. ... That is your job, you know, you new graduates with your new diplomas. Keep the plot moving. The future of humankind lies waiting for those who care about what the Badger cares about.... How to be a decent Dakotah, he tells us, is the same as how to be a good human being. How to possess tribal identity is the same as learning how to address our responsibility to all living things. I listen to the voice of the Badger and his fellow creatures and that's why I teach and write.

I want all of you to know how important your lives are, how important you are to the future of the people. I wish you much good luck in your lives. Thank you again for inviting me to this great occasion. Thanks very much and good luck to all of you. *Pidamayea.*

IV ✍ ✍ ✍

Omnipresence/Thunder

Tonant, symphonic, the providential
spirits of the land are all around me
    I'm home
from above long flat mesas of the so-called
Badlands of the Northern Plains,
themselves symbols of regeneration and
      immortality,
    low, hollow tones meet in resonance
layers of blue, shadowy blue hills
which are part of the great wall.
    I'm home
Rich and sonorous thunder is all around
the headlights of my car and its lone driver
are blurred in the fulminating
    welcome
    glittering rain, like the palpitation
    of my heart tracing
    a gentle moment falls
    in an illuminating series of open shifts

Suddenly, loudmouthed and deafening
as proficient hawks at feast, the
reverberation of the spirits
    endow sequels of lightning
    with dominion

to make my presence worthwhile
and articulate.

I'm home again.

A Mixed Marriage
2002

I crease the sheet. I hold my brush aloft.
The difference in my life since you left
is to constantly speak of the old songs
yet live for now. Now.
These morning duties are rough and open-minded,
as painful as the birthtime of fading daylight.

We were trapped in a compelling act of imagining
as we claimed the Popol Vuh. I open with
Ate oyapi, you still talk the old gambling language
of coastal waters and your People, as inland fog turns away
and fades echoing a prolonged song of our poetry and politics.

I feel your absence a betrayal of whatever it was
that tempted me to think our lives could be anything
but a biography of lost chances, a shift from
what it means to be and feel
a failure.

Writing Is a Hard Thing to Do
2002

I was born into colonialism
on an Indian Reservation

no need to describe it

I know it when I see it

I could have been a writer
but, instead, I am about politics:
you have to denounce Bush and Fiske and Rudyard Kipling
you have to denounce Costner who dances with wolves

I don't need to write if I am not going to nation build
I don't need to write if I am not going to see it as a social movement

It's odd, then, that people, not pissed-off enough at the genocidal war
going on in this country can't move in their own self-interest

    it's because we don't know our own past,
    not having read Melville and Derek Walcott

    democratizers stole the Black Hills and Crazy Horse was killed
    San Francisco's Chinatown went up in flames,
    the westward course of empire headed for the Philippines

and the hot, blank pages of history spread like amnesia
to Vietnam and Iraq

From 1900 to 1924, the years my fathers grew to manhood,
we endured incredible genocide, mass psychosis,
methods of political control, the weeding out of unwanted groups

that was before my time, as they say.

I am Nobody,
being vanished,
suffering from political obsolescence

we all got tongue-tied
after the White Treaty-Makers came
and shot Sitting Bull on the banks of the Grand River.

A Gentle Heart
for Teo and all grandsons

barren, gray limbs of a naked Chinese elm
in my front yard swing against the melancholy of an empty house
popping gusts, rattling and harassing

winds touch earth
in triumph and kneel before
the cracked horizon of your absence

cars leave the driveway

I stare past my reflection in the pain and your gentle heart
comes to the window to speak of staying away
telling me you don't like your childish life anymore

once there had been books and lasagna
your favorite dish at my kitchen table
matching your appetite for the enthusiasm
of the old '67 GMC creaking wearily in the wake of
its exhaust smoke and you were fifteen and we prayed
that nothing would change

after a while I thought of nothing
but what is at stake in your leaving

Indianist to the core, I worry
that straying from our place and our *tiospaye*
you will know nothing but the conversation of others
and your gentle heart will be wounded by a shrill life
as you go east, to the dissolute land where people crowd about.

A Poem

for Jesse

The rooms are quiet
and I'm reading the poems of

a poet you don't know
and the rooms are quiet

they are quiet because they have to be
without you, your long legs stretching

into the quiet rooms, yawning loud and near
like waiting for a door, a sound, music and talk

the rooms are quiet and sleep won't come
and I'm reading the poems about a

child's absence and Dylan Thomas and Simon
now in their middle age and a father in jail

and I don't know where you are.
The rooms are quiet.

They are quiet because they have to be
without you.

When I did graduate work

at the University of Nebraska, the first invitation I got was from
the head of the English Department to come and read poetry every
Tuesday. "Read your own," he said, "or anybody's. Emily Dickinson,
Jimmy Baca, . . . anybody." It was there I got acquainted with the work
of people like David Allen Evans, who eventually wrote stuff like

Old Racquetball Player

Down in the court stands the old player;
He is fat and bald with collapsed calves;
He is out of breath;
He asks for a time-out with raised racquet
And hung head

and became a poet laureate. He wrote a South Dakota inventory from
Kunming, China. Poems always fix landscape but that one doesn't, just
names it out of loneliness, perhaps, or remembrance. It was at the U
of Nebraska that I met Larry Holland, who had a few acres he called a
ranch and told me how to break a horse as though my brother, Victor,
hadn't told me that years ago!!!! He talked to me about the wonderful
sameness of America as though he really believed it even though he
was an avid reader of Wallace Stevens, who remarked about "a tragic
land," and Larry and I both knew what he meant.

Whatever Happened to D'Arcy McNickle?

When McNickle, the Salashan scholar, critic, and fiction writer published *Surrounded* in 1935 he was writing about real people and real events, the struggle of Indian governments, the politics of Americanism and assimilation. He presented academic scholarship, too, such as the classic *Indian Tribes of the United States: Ethnic and Cultural Survival* for the London Institute of Race Relations, a study that was published by Oxford University Press as early as 1962 and, subsequently, used in every Indian Studies course worth mentioning. He did not write much poetry, so far as we know.

His fictional novel, *Surrounded,* along with the other fictions he published, did not garner the attention his academic work did, which means, one supposes, that only in American Indian Literary Studies can a writer of novels be ignored because he is also a scholar, analyst, researcher, and politically inclined. Yet his fiction found a brief audience about a dozen years ago when it was contrasted with the newest work of Indian sophisticates who rose out of the acclaimed university creative writing departments.

Though Native American Literary Study in fiction is such a broad field, the contemporary novel seems now to be the most visible genre used in schools and universities, and it is used, purportedly, to teach all manner of history, politics, sociology, and creativity concerning American Indian life and affairs. Unlike the realistic fiction of D'Arcy McNickle, though, which required that roots, legacy, and geographies be the central focus for the imaginative works, most of the contemporary novels emerging today as popular venues for study do just the opposite. I would argue that the clear message in the most visible of the new American Indian novels, those works published in the last decade or so, is that it is important to escape roots and legacies and geographies rather than center upon them as the McNickle works do, even while the writers imagine them in ironic and sophisticated ways. The reasons are numerous, I suppose, but one of the reasons is that these legacies are too filled with anguish. I've thought about all of this as I've gone about my casual reading of such exemplars as *The Heartsong of Charging Elk*, by James Welch, and *The Bingo Palace*, by Louise Erdrich. Both of these fictions, I think, illustrate my point.

The path to literary notice in the Native American literary field these days is to tell endless stories about fractured, landless families, or to examine native characters doing out-of-this-world things in the mode of magic realism, or surrealism. Writers, transforming and liberating the unconscious, tell fantastic stories about the deficit lives of urban Indians on the streets of America, or the anguish of living lives of poverty and despair on the homelands. The flourishing message is that one must escape one's roots, despair over their loss, but escape, escape, escape. How? By particularly engaging in magical and endless discussions of spider webs and mixed bloods and lost hopes.

James Wood, a British literary critic, whose work appears regularly in such places as the *London Review of Books*, published a piece not too long ago in which he observed this trend in worldwide novel writing, so it is, perhaps, not just a trend in the imaginative works of American Indian writers. It is Wood's assertion that the need to escape roots in fiction is much more important than the reality that one came to expect when one read the novels of thirty years ago. The vision most novelists of today have, Wood says, is that real lives either aren't interesting enough or relevant enough for publishers to prepare them for public consumption and editors, he says, seem to go along with the trend toward magic realism, surrealism, or any of the other transformative techniques in vogue at this time. Even the early fictionist, Momaday, one may observe, in *House Made of Dawn*, utilized stream-of-consciousness techniques in character development some twenty years ago, an influential technique perfected by the Freudian Bloomsbury groups in England. It is important to observe that Wood isn't talking about E. L. Doctorow, whose interest in and use of history in novels like *The Book of Daniel* were most profound, and he is not talking, either, about Saul Bellow and Philip Roth, both notable exceptions to this trend.

Wood's point, though, that novels have abandoned storytelling techniques in favor of magic realism and spectacle is as important to native writers as it is to any other writers. Wood is afraid that novels have simply become perpetual motion, caricature, and hysterical magic realism, and he examines several features of character and plot as evidence: always the great rock musician appears who, when born-again, began "immediately to play air guitar in his crib" (Rushdie); a talking dog, a mechanical duck, a giant octagonal cheese, and two clocks having a conversation (Pynchon); a nun called Sister Edgar who is obsessed with germs and who may be a reincarnation of J. Edgar Hoover (Pynchon); a conceptual artist painting retired B-52 bombers in the New Mexico desert (DeLillo); a terrorist group called Wheelchair Assassins devoted to the liberation of Quebec (DeLillo); and a film so compelling that anyone who sees it dies (Foster Wallace). Another example Wood cites features a Jewish scientist who is genetically engineering a mouse (we don't know why), a group of Jehovah's Witnesses who think the world is ending (I guess they've always thought that), and twins, one in Bangladesh and one in London, who both break their noses at the same time, no rationale, no explanation (Wallace).

Wood asks the quintessential question: what does it all mean in terms of literature in a society and its contribution to civilization? This is not an unworthy question, and it is particularly relevant to the reorganization of Indian lives at the turn of the century when it would appear that great, large, land-based tribal nations in America mean to survive their decades-long struggle for sovereign status. It is hard to say what one can assume from this trend of escaping roots, but it is, perhaps, safe to conclude that the conventions of realism where roots are essential, are being not only distorted or abolished, as occurs in magic realism, but, as Wood asserts, they are in literature simply being exhausted and overworked.

These modern writers are simply trying too hard, Wood asserts. "It is not a question of objecting to this trend of escaping roots because of a lack of verisimilitude, which is the usual charge against botched realism," he broods, "this kind of writing cannot be faulted because it lacks reality, but, rather, because it is evasive of reality." Its purpose is to evade reality, Wood asserts, reiterating that "its purpose is to escape roots and real humanity and real character development." All of this is very convincing, yet, Woods just doesn't tell us WHY.

Examining the characters of modern American Indian fiction, I agree with Wood's assessment, but the explanations for why this is so seem much more obvious in Native American stories than in the mainstream ones. We know why the rock musician comes to the Spokane Indian Reservation in the enormously popular Sherman Alexie work *Reservation Blues.* It is to vitalize, to give life to a dead, staid, dull native culture that no longer has any relevance to the people or to the world, to place new roots in the soil of a caricatured place where the roots of reality aren't just "buried too damn deep," as Wood suggests. They are dead.

Other examples might seem more ambiguous, as concerns roots and identities, but are, still, discernable. In a Gordon Henry novel, *Light People*, for example, a character speaks only in Haiku and some drunks try to repatriate a severed leg that has been frozen and is now floating down the river. In Louise Erdrich, characters are full of strangeness. One woman character, I think it is Fleur in *Tracks*, goes about with a severed finger in her apron pocket but, again, we don't know why. When I taught a largely non-Indian class in NA Literatures at UC Davis a few years ago, some students were convinced it was some kind of traditional Ojibway practice of medicine women. In *Bearheart*, by Gerald Vizenor, there is all manner of curious behavior and events that we can expect because the novel is set in a post—nuclear war period, the point being that in this new world order there can not only be no roots, there can be no morals nor ethics either. In Momaday's new work, Set goes mad and is recovered through Bear spirit. Young Bear joins in by saying: "I once envisioned my mind as a burly porcupine magnificent in its body armor protected by long, fire-hardened spikes."

Speaking of porcupines (while this is veering off a bit from the subject at hand), one finds the starving Oglalas of *The Heartsong of Charging Elk* out on the Stronghold in the late 1800s eating porcupine soup that would, in reality, be something like eating their horses or each other, an activity they would consider so offensive as to be indecent. In reality, Oglalas never ate porcupine. He was called *pahin* and even when they wanted to rip off his quills and hair for their own dress styles and accoutrements they never killed him, let alone made a meal of him. This complaint concerning verisimilitude probably does not belong in this discussion except that a knowledgeable reader finds it difficult to move on when struck by such lack of cultural authenticity or realism. In this work, too, Oglalas are boiling their moccasins for soup, which is a contrived historical activity perpetuated by seventeenth-century observers who recorded this activity in ethnographic writings and called it traditional, cultural behavior.

There is little or no significant corroboration of this activity, but, in a very recent work, *Books and Islands in Ojibwe Country* (Washington, D.C.: National Geographic Directions, 2003), Louise Erdrich gives an unwitting example of where this falsity might have come from. She refers to the 1789 captive narrative by John Tanner with the lengthy title *The Falcon: A Narrative of the Captivity and Adventures of John Tanner During Thirty Years Residence among the Indians in the Interior of North America*, from which she gives her readers this information (p. 45), "At the leanest times, Tanner's family was forced to *boil and eat their own moccasins,* to subsist on the inner bark of trees or dead vines." She tells us that Tanner was one of those early explorers of Indian Country with the Indian name Shaw-shaw-wa-Be-na-se, or Falcon, and was said to have been a captive of the Shawnee, sold to the Ojibway, and from then on was said to have lived entirely as an Ojibway. Erdrich is a steadfast fan of Tanner's writings and sees herself in his world. When she shares his stories with her sister Lise, they agree that Tanner "vanished into his own legend." They both are in love with this captive narrative, comparing it to *The Adventures of Huckleberry Finn*, suggesting it is a compelling history of the region. Erdrich's final remark is, "As he was to all respects a 'white Indian,' and saw the world as an Ojibwe, his is the first narrative of native life from an Ojibwe point of view" (p. 46).

It may be possible that this kind of attempt at validating the "oral traditions," which is one of the major thrusts of the entire *Books and Islands* manuscript, creates an ethic and a history that blend themselves with the traditional customs of indigenous peoples until it is difficult to say how these personal writing have melded early "white Indian" observations with indigenous behaviors and customs. This is hardly an example of "escaping roots," but it may be an example of creating new ones.

There may be other points to be made concerning authenticity of contemporary works, but the fact that Charging Elk in Welch's novel becomes Francois and never goes home again is probably the most salient point to be made concerning the message about the need to escape roots. Welch, we are told, researched a real-life character, even traveling to France to find him in an historical setting, an author's technique in fiction that is meant to give this message and its interpretation authenticity. There is no question that such events of relocation occurred. It is well documented by white historians that some Oglalas and other Indians of the nineteenth century participated in the "wild west shows" and Buffalo Bill extravaganzas depicted in this fiction and it is a fact that some of them did not return to their homelands. Thus, there can be no complaint of a lack of verisimilitude or authenticity. But Wood's point, that fiction writers focus on the message that roots and the return to them no longer represent a viable center for character development, is given substance here, and it is up to the critic to speculate on the reasons for that focus.

In the Welch manuscript, it is clear that Charging Elk embodies the "vanishing American" theory so well known in Indian history. He is obliterated as an Oglala. The odd thing about this novel is that it is thought to be historical realism when, in fact, very few Oglalas had this experience, and it is, therefore, hardly a realistic and significant portrayal of native life. Charging Elk is an anomaly as are the few Oglalas who are said to have had this experience. To read this life as an examination of the realities of the period is probably a mistake, since other historical events of the period present the more salient environment in which character development must occur. For example, in 1877, the Black Hills were stolen from the people by congressional fiat, condemning them to poverty, early death and disease; the Major Crimes Act was passed in 1883 when Crow Dog shot Spotted Tail and the result was the curtailing of their rights to sovereign nationhood; in December 1890, Sitting Bull (who had participated in the Buffalo Bill shows as exemplified by Charging Elk but returned home, as did most of these warriors, to defend the people and the land) was shot to death by federal police at his place on the Grand River; Red Cloud renegotiated the survival of the Oglalas in the 1868 Fort Laramie Treaty after having fought for a decade out on the Powder River, finally settling his people at the White River. Though some of this is implied in the Welch story, there is little real encapsulation of the history of the brutalization of the American Indian in this critical period or in the characterization of Charging Elk. It is not only a disappointing read to those who have come to think that art can contribute to social criticism, but it is convincing evidence of the avoidance Wood examines.

Turning back to that point made by literary critic Wood, Charging Elk does escape his roots and seems glad to have done so. At the conclusion of the story, still curiously bewildered by the turn his life has taken, Charging Elk is content in his marriage to a French woman, his roots dead and unlamented. He has escaped the reality of being an Oglala in the modern world. He, among a select few, has had an unusual experience of displacement, which is what, perhaps, makes him a subject for contemporary fiction. As a fictionalized character he seems confused, yet resolved. The curious bewilderment displayed by this character seems to give substance to the idea that this is a clear case of sacrificing a character to the message.

Wood goes even further to say that "the evasion of reality, while borrowing from reality, itself, is a cover-up." It covers up, he contends, the notion that roots matter in this modern world or that they are even accessible. In the case of the American Indian novel of the last decade, the questions of what it is that authors are "covering up" is curiously unexamined. It is true that native writers of today are several generations removed from war or brutal colonization or enforced assimilation or even the memory of exile.

It is true that the present scene is two hundred years distant from treaty-signing and Wounded Knee and the Powder River Wars and the Removal of the Tribes and the Long Walk of the Dine and the theft of a continent. It is true, also, that memories of such events are equally distant from old languages and values and customs stemming from a long-ago way of life. Perhaps those roots and legacies are buried too deep and that is the reason the "cover-up" or the "evasion" is so tempting to current writers. It's easier not to have to claim it at all. It is easier to become someone separated from his country, and imagine a new nontribal ego.

Yet for those who find such a rationale unconvincing, there is still the explanation that to exile one's self from one's history as a fictionist is a personal choice that may have severe consequences beyond personal ones. Writers several generations removed from roots and legacies are, often, expected by an assimilationist public to exhibit a personal, self-imposed hysteria of the imagination ending in a kind of expatriation. By law and national U.S. policy, indigenous peoples all over the continent as well as those in other countries plagued by colonizationist histories, have been removed from their specific geographic homelands, displaced in a thousand different ways, and developed into permanent expatriation status. Is the consequence of that a significant rationale to examine?

Wole Soyinka, for example, the Nigerian writer now living in the United States, thinks so. He suggests that the condition of the third-world writer in exile "is that of a telephone person, in touch with the world but with no world to call his own." Because of the nonvoluntary nature of this displacement, some (but not Soyinka) have suggested that there may be no other alternative. Assuming for a moment that the American Indian writer can be seen as an exile, the world he or she creates in the imagination can certainly be a world without roots. While on the telephone, a singularly isolating instrument of technology, one can give credibility to all manner of rumor, exaggeration, lies, traumas. It is my contention that D'Arcy McNickle, even though he spent much of his professional life in Washington, D.C., and Chicago, and other cities of America, refused the imagination of the exile position and remained, in his own image, a tribal person in touch with his tribal compatriots. It is my contention, also, that many of the sophisticated native writers who came after McNickle, have not.

If exile is a real cause for the moving away from realistic fiction into the hysterical nature of the magically realistic stories being told now, the future of Native American fiction remains in question. Will it continue to be the spectacle it has become in the last decade, a sprouting of bazaar and deformed imaginings that made tragedy and anguish irrelevant or, worse, a silly joke? Or will it approach characters and make them human in an intelligent balance of family, sex, war, history, life, memory of the past, and vitality? Real humanity in characterization is what is at stake here.

To arrive at exile as a writer, according to Soyinka, at least, is a matter of choice. One must say, "I have arrived at Exile," and go on from there into taking whatever role is useful to interpretation. If the loss is too anguishing, the surreal imagination is a way out. If cultural longing is overwhelming, suicide and the end of history and the end of character become the function of plot. If we take literature seriously, though, we must know that as histories and writers are defeated in this way, the pages of human recall become empty and this is dangerous for the whole world.

The need to escape human memory and roots is something that can be sacrificed to magic and the marketplace if the only responsibility of literature is to popularly embrace the barriers to reality that should not be there in the first place. To embrace the unreal spectacle of the Buffalo Bill fantasy, as one must do if one is to respond emotionally to Charging Elk, is to give up on the notion that reality and history matter. A literature that succeeds on the threshold of reality but accepts the surreal or fantastic in order to keep in touch, however tangentially, with the chaotic and nontribal world that is moving on with or without either the reader or the writer, suggests the end of storytelling and the beginning of fairy tales.

The chasm between the works of the Montana Salishan writer/ historian D'Arcy McNickle and the newest American Indian novelists may widen. Thus, the question of what the need to escape roots means and what the current novelists are evading in the new fiction may boil down to the private expression of themes and ideas of *permanent exile*. The radical renaissance of the 1960s will be over and I, for one, will no longer consider the creation of contemporary Native American literary art a cause for rejoicing.

Going Away

from dusty towns we pass crowds of weekend shoppers
whose grandfathers threatened Northern Indians with
the destruction of their women and children

who took it upon themselves to appoint
head chiefs for the Menominees, the
Dakotahs, Omahas, and Oglalas, placing medals
around their necks, blinding them with
absurd gibberish. It's almost September.
I look in the side mirror at rough surface
streets, like the Zócalo in Mexico City where
bureaucrats and farmers gather in straw hats
and tourists pack the town square to watch
the marketeers in cowboy boots, yellow leaves
say time passes, and I hope for the fall chill
to erase those names from streets
that campaign still for shrewd deal-making
land thieves who publicly praise us for being Indians.

Shadows follow my car into the hills
I pass a cemetery of bones, a hidden hunting knife
carried westward lying beside the skeleton so long gone,
ditches filled with scrap iron, patches of brush lining lighted
parking lots outside of town. I pass by the Gutzon Borglum
Museum while *Winning the West* author/politician
stares down from the sacred mountain.

When Scott Momaday,

the Kiowa, wrote *Way to Rainy Mountain* and his first novel, *House Made of Dawn*, he used a mirror to reflect the rise of the NCAI and, without really wanting to, wrote to protest the white supremacy and incredible genocide of public policy that had happened during those years prior to his birth. He is a genuinely brilliant artist whose classic novel is inspired by politics, like the work of Arthur Miller, whose drama *The Crucible*, used the seventeenth-century Salem, Massachusetts, story to reflect the policy of Senator Joseph McCarthy's "witch hunts" in the United States in the 1950s.

What is at stake in both works is the sense of the survival of the village and the tribe.

V ∂∂∂

The Riverpeople

Red Cloud always said his Oglalas
did not want to live on the Missouri River.

They wanted to live thirty miles east of Fort Laramie
on the Platte. No Heart said the white man had
already ruined the Missouri River so that
no Indian could live there. The Unktechis,
he said, were now afraid. That's how Fort Robinson
became a place of death and destruction. They say this.

The Isianti were sent up there in boats
as prisoners from the Little Crow War.
So were the Yanktons and Winnebagos.

Later, Corn Woman told them all
that she would live there as one of the wives

of the buffalo.

September 5/2004

"A basic attribute of colonialism lies in the way 'conquerors' control how history is told and perpetuated." This sentence is an exact quote from a lovely professor of literature I've known for several decades. It is nothing new, just real. The professor tells us that study of the diaries of "discoverers" from the time of Marco Polo to the present is much admired and an ongoing literary phenomena.

In the rain at Eagle Butte, I was thinking about this phenomenon as I hurriedly approached a magnificent white tent, and I looked about with some regard at sidings of life-size drawings by the eighteenth-century artist George Catlin of himself and Meriwether Lewis and William Clark and Sacajawea and Charbonneau, even York, fur traders and mountain men, all controllers of history. Inside the tent were Indians "telling our own stories," with alert National Park Service guides lining the aisles and ushering people to their seats. The Indian storytellers told who their relatives were. This day was the anniversary of the killing of Crazy Horse one hundred thirty-seven years ago, yet no one mentioned his name.

Here, Lakota persons have always associated places with particular ancestors yet now they speak of them within the exploits of two white men who called themselves "explorers," men who paid no attention to the epistemology of words, men who drove home the notion that "discovery" of Indians would influence a U.S. National Indian policy of Genocide for the next two hundred years. Coming through the fluvial landscape of the Missouri River from the Black Hills to Eagle Butte casts a spell for the endangered and vanishing ones, and my takoja speaks my thoughts: "We're ALONE here, aren't we, *unchida*."

I couldn't answer. There has always been a lot of talk associated with the Lewis and Clark story about "the end of history." Indeed, Francis Fukuyama, a member of the federal government's bioethics council, has recently written something about *the end of history and the last man,* an intriguing and obscene thought palpable with fear.

The reason to care about this end-of-history idea is because we are now at the beginning of a new century, governed by antihistorical neoconservatives who have begun an enormous first-strike war in the Middle East with dire consequences for the entire globe. It's no longer just "us" Indians and "those" white folks. Now, it is the entire Arab and Muslim world pitted against the Christian and Jewish colonizers. But, of course, the end-of-history idea is nothing new to Americans. Ever since Frederick Jackson Turner wrote his "frontier thesis" and declared the indigenous peoples of this continent a mere "stage" in human development, such ideas have flourished.

For the previously mentioned literary professor and for myself (both of us naturally concerned with the end of certainty as regards language and mimesis), what is now called (in scholarly lexicon) "postmodernism" connotes a kind of finality that may be the logical extension of Turner. History and literature make an important and fearful connection.

How much should we care about all of this? There was an old Indian man, once, who could, perhaps, tell us how we need to take it all in. He was talking to an old white man who wanted to impress him, an Indian, with his land holdings as a white man who lived along the Missouri, how large his ranch was, how much property he owned. "You have to drive al-l-l day across my place," the white man said, gesturing, "and then you drive all-l-l-l night!! And even then," he went on, "you have to drive half the next day!!!"

"O-hanh," the old Indian man said, nodding his head. "I had a car like that once."

What irony!! What it means, one supposes, is that the old Indian man was not impressed with the bragging of the old white guy, and we can surmise all kinds of reasons for his offhandedness. The truth is, Indians are generally not all that impressed, either, with what may be called "postmodernism," nor with the Lewis and Clark Story, nor with Catlin's "vanishing American" paintings.... But, because the white man is impressed with himself and his accomplishments, we all gather in white tents across the wide Missouri country to listen to tall tales told by both sides. It is my perception that we are all fools for getting together to do this thing every time the forest service people want to retell their history; they are, after all, people who have stolen more Indian land than most of the white bureaucrats and politicians and land swindlers you ever knew. But, here we are, September 2004, listening to the stories of and about the greatest image makers of the West, neither tourists nor visitors.

We are introduced to one another and it is said that this is to be a gathering of "mutual discovery." The essential question is posed: "Aren't these stories of these great 'adventurers' simply INVALUABLE? Isn't the story of the Lewis and Clark Journey and the subsequent photos of the great George Catlin's paintings just PRECIOUS?!!" A museum curator spoke these exact words to me over the telephone not too long ago. The answer is: No. Of course not. Unless you want to perpetuate the Noble Red Man, The Vanishing American, the Savage stereotypes. These stories and photos are propaganda useful to disguise the real intent of the journey. It was not a journey of benign discovery, let alone a "mutual" one. It was an illegal invasion of sovereign country sponsored by the inchoate U.S. Government,

and it resulted in death to thousands of Indians, the destruction
of indigenous religious thought concerning the land, the theft of a
continent from Peoples who had lived here for many centuries, and the
degradation of an environment so sensuous that traditional medicine
men wept when they spoke of it. The Catlin and Lewis and Clark
intrusion has meant a legacy of Death to those who met them on the
Missouri River in 1804. And no one should forget that the Teton Sioux
were called "the vilest miscreants of the human race," by the selfsame
intrepid explorers.

The question, however, "Aren't these Lewis and Clark stories and
the Catlin photos simply invaluable," presupposes that the genocidal
diminishment of the indigenous life posed in them is simply gone
forever and to be mourned. We are to grieve for the passing of a noble
people.

I'm tired of grief.

I want new definitions and I want new language used to describe
this colonial genocide disguised as benign and mutual discovery.

Any Indian historian and most colonial historians will tell you
that such images and stories as those of Catlin and Lewis and Clark
are closely connected to the use of arms, the military to conquer and
subdue. That's why Helen Hunt Jackson wrote *The Century of Dishonor*,
detailing those early years even before 1830 to 1930, because it was
her perception that the Indian was being destroyed by those who
were building the greatest democracy known to man, and there was
something gone terribly wrong.

Thus, we must ask: What good are these images and stories in
2004 in the face of the massive destruction that has taken place? They
are self-serving. They serve the imperialistic intention of America.
"Well," the rejoinder is, "if you know their traits and if you know

the kindness of people like Catlin, you know that Catlin, especially, approached Indians with respect!" Of course! All cultures respect Death, even those that are the handmaidens of colonialism and imperialism. Ultimately, then, the images and photos are employed by America for the myth of generous and benign and earthly America.

They are dangerous myths. We are fools for thinking otherwise.

Irony's Blade

The study of literature and such literary techniques as the use of irony gives clues as to how the story achieves broad meanings and influences. *The politics of Irony is dangerous to the status quo. It is tricky. And it must be conceived as emancipation.*

The use of irony in art, literature, and scholarship is a political stance of great power. It is much too frequently dismissed as self-negating and self-contradicting, but it is neither just a "put-down," nor is it just negative rhetoric.

The American Indian's relationship to the Colonizer has always been an ironic one. Thus, the American Indian's response to the quincentennial literature of the Lewis and Clark journey defines itself much as the old Indian man in the previous story defines it, but also as an understanding of what we may call "the function of Image." What that response tells you is that the saga at the heart of the West cannot be interpreted as a trustworthy function of democracy or an idea of "mutual discovery," both ideas being imaginatively touted during the beginning of the twenty-first century as the American metaphor or allegory for a just and humane world.

Whether that is so or whether it is not, the Image of The White American Male as Fearless Explorer and Conqueror, intrepid, strong and brave Seeker of New Vistas going out fearlessly into the Unknown, is well established in story and legend. Why else was *Star Trek* the most popular television show in the history of the small screen? Going where no man has gone before is imagistically a given in American stories. It is so pervasive that it has now become iconic, the subject of reruns and satire.

If you think this imagistic icon is over, a thing of the past, a remnant of a once-courageous history to be referred to as nostalgic remembrance, think again. Harry Potter has emerged as the most recent Seeker of the **Unknown**. Kids of all ages read it eagerly and the story ends up on the *New York Times* Best Seller list as the best book of the period. It remains there for months on end. It is a good thing, we are told by everyone, except those Christians who worry about witchcraft, the same Christians who called Indians "savages." It is no wonder us skins are schizophrenic.

It is clear, though, that most Americans buy into the basic premises of the Lewis and Clark Saga, however one argues about the real intent. They are as follows:

1. The journey into the Unknown is a good and inevitable thing.
2. White America has the duty and responsibility to bring its ideas and values into the Unknown because they are good.
3. These ideas and values will be welcomed because they are good.
4. Religiosity is the guiding force and should be shared with others, all mankind.

Isn't it ironic, then, that most American Indians, the very subjects against which the protagonists of "discovery" interact, fail to accept the basic premises of the Lewis and Clark Saga? Let's call it "ironic" instead of "protestation" because at the end of the twentieth century, lamentations, protests, and oppositional modes of scholarship are everywhere in the Indian-White story, and protest literatures are thought to be inferior genres. Let's drag it all kicking and screaming into the "literary" scene. Perhaps there is a serious reason for the irony of rejection. From the Indian's point of view, there is no "Unknown" in the geographic sense that Lewis and Clark remark upon. To the indigenous figure, there is nothing in this world that is "Unknown" in the sense that it must be sought out, "discovered," claimed, and exploited. The indigenous thought on this is that there are indigenous environments everywhere, on the next street, there where the neighboring tribes live, in the next town, on the moon, and in the universe. Indigenousness is a real and ubiquitous thing, not mysterious and "Unknown." Indeed, isn't it ironic that even Harry Truman, that old dropper of atomic bombs, told us that there is nothing new in history ... only the history you don't know?! He was right, of course. It is ironic, then, that America's intrepid explorer suggests otherwise and sees his works flourish among the puritans.

Only in colonizing worlds of European nations, it would seem, is exploring, invading, and occupying "Unknown" places universally admired, which means that the above-named four tenets are put forward with a straight face and embraced with much enthusiasm. There are even great philosophers to back up the colonizers' point of view. Do not protest through Irony, they tell us, because "the ironist is a vampire." Søren Kierkegaard tells us this and says that irony is a vampire "who has sucked the blood out of her lover and fanned him with coolness, lulled him to sleep and tormented him with turbulent firearms." All subsequent writers, until just recent times, agreed that irony was dangerous to the status quo and should be feared as liberation.

We are not talking, here, about sarcasm or wit or humor or tongue-in-cheek irony. We are speaking to the serious, literary, and historical use of irony. The white explorers who met the Teton Sioux on the Missouri River in 1804 called them uncomplimentary names, yet claimed, used, and exploited their customs, attire, and lands for their own benefit. In the same way, the ironist is called names by philosophers, yet history and literature and philosophy all conspire to claim his propensity for the purpose of preventing or engendering an oppositional rhetoric.

The Tetons were called "the vilest miscreants of the human race" simply because they were telling Lewis and Clark: "We will control the traffic on this river, and you are unwelcome intruders," something the intruders did not want to hear. The Indians, as protesters, then, were called nasty names in the same way and for the same reasons that the historian named them savages, which is ironic since they were not any more "savage" than the colonists who called them that.

The hatred of the use of Irony stems from the notion that in the end, irony is not just a trope or a discursive strategy. Instead, it is a device that helps you tell an unsuspecting audience what you really mean.

Democracy in 2002 and the Free Press

A disputed election
a pretender president

press coverage
like a flood shrouds circumstances
of political theft, journals stride past in fear
and darkness, faded shawls about their shoulders

but, the fcc changes its regulations
so news organizations
can become conglomerates
ravenous, sanctimonious abusers
of the rights of mankind.

We are witness to no miracles
the water grows thick with fallen
cottonwoods and dogs lapping along
the shore drop dead from swift infections.

The unsuspected bacteria of unknowable tidal traffic
unleashed by the river crews locating and clearing
centuries of growth and estuaries
rides a quick current to villages
and towns along the shore

where are the lifeboats of history?

Murder at the Nebraska Line

Here are two homeless Indian men walking North from
White Clay, and to the South is a village of twenty-two
white folks stalled in a hundred years of Realism,
stone blue sky, and a hot prairie wind. Here is another
corpse, no, two, falling at random: from the only horse
to survive the Battle or like a god too close to the sun.

Some call it America, some call it Star Wars, some call it
docu-dramas interrupting geographies of hope by Ken Burns.
Well, they were heroes, weren't they?

This day, stretching into a night of straight shots, is an
improvisation that gives off light for just this moment,
but they're History, and the memory of Battle, or Massacre,
or Myth shapes and tears apart their love for themselves.
They weren't even born then and now there's no one
to break their fall. Here are two homeless Indian men
walking north from White Clay.

Change

(looking at 1888 photo of a hundred Sioux Indians and
Gen. Pratt in Washington, D.C.)

1

I see a man stalking them on a cold cement step

not looking at anything but the nameless camera man
uninterrupted by such little things as poetry or song,
a nearly human glare in his eyes, he is confident as the one chosen
to deal from a stacked deck, in the discreet era of choice:
assimilation or extinction.[1]

All his life he defended his role: kill the Indian, save the man.
then died without ceremony in the year his victims became U.S.
citizens

annual rituals of his dream, spitting the dialect of genocidal
converts and mindless idlers, played out at Carlisle for four decades
in dramatic games of yesterday, but there he stands, hands at the ready

2

His child's hymn book left on the steps of a rotting government,[2]
he was a crusader as much as a soldier, a maker of men

1. "Indians are to go upon said reservations ... they have no alternative but to
choose between this policy and extermination." 1868. 40th Congress.
2. Helen Hunt Jackson called these years of Pratt's influence the century of
dishonor.

in his own image, a born-again reformer with no faith in heaven.
It was the Army. It was the Army. He called Custer "the flower" and
worried about the "trembling" of "our women and children" on the
frontiers and, then, for the sake of humanity, accepted the Indians as
"brothers" to make them in his image.

3

There was his Lakota student, Plenty Horses, who shot Lt. E. W. Casey
in 1891[3] in order to wipe away the blot of Carlisle, there was the
old man, resisting Empire, shaking his cane at the killers at
    Manderson,
mute in 1888, cradling his pipe, two years before the sun dims,
there was a shadowy sparrow flitting on the 17th Street Mall in Denver,
talking
in a language no one knew, about the honor dance they would do more
    than
a hundred years later, calling it celebratory, at the National Museum.
    An omen.

4

at the Minneluzaha,[4]
thin water rushed over the
the bones of women and children
who failed the test of Thanksgiving

---

3. This event took place after the massacre at Wounded Knee.
4. The Lakota name of a rapid creek (a swiftwater) in the Black Hills.

there was no milk and honey there

only intoxicating liquor
sold by fur traders
and given freely at every stop
by the "Journeyers."[5]

The crusader writes from the Carlisle Barracks
to the Quaker friend giving $800,
"Now I have steam heat for the boys' quarters,"
to keep them suitable prisoners another year
in Pennsylvania. Far from the
sun they left behind in the rightful places,
they abandoned Bad River at the mouth of the Missouri.
In drafty classrooms they drifted along corridors
in dark afternoons.

5

The old ones heard the century move with malice
toward a showdown and saw their
sons become strange and melancholy.
Spotted Tail had talked "offensively"
about the school and had removed his heirs.
The sky, awkward and coarse
like the tireless wind, welcomed them
and separate silences dissolved

5. Reference to Lewis and Clark.

their imaginations of themselves
forever changed.

Carlisle was located in an unpainted world
unimpeachable in its righteousness
giving things their names and rearranging
lives growing gaunt and pale, forever changed; in
imitation, they copied and mimicked, without heart
they returned to the homelands and the old crusader
bit the dust thinking he would become Stonewall Jackson.

October 2004

It is unfortunate that our most profound native intellectual, N. Scott Momaday, did not live in the time when writers were romantics, when they were promised fame and glamour with the notion that they would become venerable in their last decades. He should have lived in the time of mid-seventeenth-century romanticism, a period of the fabulous, the extravagant, the fictitious, and the unreal; you know, before Defoe and Journalism, before Oscar Wilde and the moderns. Instead, he is a writer who lives in a "fallen time" in literary studies, yet claims not to be interested in politics, only the story. Often, he disappoints many of his readers when he fails to be disreputable and fails to answer the forced and expected political questions, and follow the sociology of the protests of "his people" so much in the forefront of the twentieth-century narrative.

In Portland, Oregon, the other day, he told his audience, "Lewis and Clark remains in my mind one of the great epic odysseys in American history," and the newspaper correspondent from the *Indian Voice* bemoaned his generous spirit by asking, "Where is the militancy? Where is the rhetoric about how the coming of Lewis and Clark spelled the demise of traditional tribal life and thus Indian people have no reason to laud the occasion?" How can he say, "We must stand in awe of them"? How can he shake his white mane of hair and say, "We welcomed them to our world. We gave them melons"?

This is a writer who holds the post of Regent's Professor of Humanities at the University of Arizona and in 1969 won a Pulitzer Prize for his novel *House Made of Dawn.* I've been a devoted fan of this writer for years and have cherished the idea that his writing received such a substantial award as the Pulitzer, but, frankly, on this one, I'm with the news reporter. Momaday's awestruck pose concerning Lewis and Clark may be over the top, for me. The Pulitzer is, as you know, the "people's prize," a famous one with considerable prestige, but now I have to ask, "what people?" "whose people?" Who is on the panel of judges that awards such prizes? Indians? Probably not. Joseph Pulitzer said this, when he began this prize giving: "Annually, for the American novel published during the year which shall best present the whole atmosphere of American life and the highest standard of American manners and manhood. $1,000." *Gone With the Wind* got it in 1937 for suggesting that slaves were happy and without guile, James Michener's *Tales of the South Pacific* got it ten years later for describing romantic interludes in a land of strife, and Oliver LaFarge got it in 1931, which makes you wonder if the same panelists were rewarding the same hokey stories for the same hokey tastes. Thomas Wolfe got it most recently for telling us, among other things, we can't go home again. Truth is, I haven't followed the Pulitzer, lately, but I believe the poet Eavan Boland said it best: "Writers are not rewarded for failing to engage a substantial audience." Well, in spite of my ambiguity about politics and prose, it doesn't change my opinion about *House Made of Dawn*. It is a classic and should be studied in every classroom in America.

At Churchside, 1995

His long, strange odyssey finally ended,
death came, but this is not a eulogy.

The wind blew all the dark night, winter
so cold it cracked the bark on trees. I sat in
underheated rooms perspiring, firm in
false decency, calloused to ill fate and threat,
the frosted glass on windows making designs
that plead and agonize on every failure.

A very sick man drew his last breath
and the little Indian town where he was
buried in the white-man forgiving way
was, as they say around here,
froze-up.

Afterwards, I sat with others in a
dank tavern, a shrine to making excuses,
laughing too loud through my rage,
drinking dark wine.

Contradictions: Good Intentions from a Nation That Loves You

the first Nobel Prize
was given thirty years ago
by a man who invented dynamite,
the first solid nitroglycerin, and it became
an annual symbol of achievement in America.

no one really remembers who he was
did he have a wife?
do his children love him?
he was a significant
contributor to America's tradition of
respecting the gun and dynamite

we left, after all,
twenty-one million bomb craters
in Vietnam

to be born in America is to
dream of transformation

it is a double place to be
a contested place to be
to find the way to America
is to be drawn to catastrophe:
the Peace and Freedom Party

was organized in 1968
after Malcolm was shot
and Robert and Martin Luther King

A Lakota tomb lies quiet in the sun
at Wounded Knee
a double place, a contested place

....

love often kills the dream
and we love America ....

A Commutative Poem about Graduate School

Shakespeare did not flatter
the monarch and has been sold out
for four hundred years

I've tried not to forget that
as I mix another screwdriver

I wanted to be a poet
but there was no scholarship
for poetry

unless you wrote heartland
poems that flattered the moral principles
of western civ

I was asked to take the Rorschach,
the thematic apperception test,
a sentence completion test
and the Minnesota Multiphasic Personality Index

scoring high on the Miller's Analogy,

I swore, drunkenly or sweetly,
I'd write between the lines
responding to my aching heart's echo
of when whole generations hid
in green darkness

Exile

(Homage to Wole Soyinka)

I carve a star apple as I get ready for his reading
the sun darkens oleanders along the parkway

Why here? Reno, Nevada?

"Anguish," he says, "goes into the surreal imagination,"
drowning in old ways the real thing. I tire of the
condition of the exile, which is the subject of his talk.
the metaphor, its ambiguity, its self-love: the telephone person,
in touch with all the world but no world to call his own.

Students screech in hallways
the best minds babbling
I trudge this sunlit stair
to a thunderous sound
fading to silence
in my wounded heart.

We all write from isolated enclaves
not choosing such things
as cultural longing, barriers, loss of memory
it is not self-imposed, this existential alienation
rather it is the blow of dictators, colonists, and Puritans

One day, tear gas scatters the demonstration,
flaring like the raising of that alien flag at White River
and we are in custody again at Lagos and Denver
ads for pioneer lands and bank accounts
for oil and gold economies around the world
expose the first sales of indigenous assets
from Baghdad and Cairo to Yankton and Albuquerque.

Colonial literatures call us "defeated" nations,
doomed, on the threshold of reality,
described as open sores or locations of trauma
driving the native artist toward the past,
nostalgically, ending in self-discovery
and ultimate disillusion.

Ever since the Red Indian and other tribes
of the large continents met with colonizers
there has developed a dialogue concerning war,
disaster, displacement, the exercise of power, the
struggle for tribal survival, autonomy, sovereignty
suggesting the displaced person, facing
outside forces meant to converge and occupy
and takeover, must be in a permanent state of exile.

His hair, wiry as last year's tinsel, a halo
brazenly fine as dark cocoa bushes
blares noon or twilight in the spotlight
behind the podium: "I have not arrived,"

he said then, "at exile. Not at a place of surreal
tension, rather, a place of reality."

He was
arrested four years later, in Nigeria's commercial capital
Saturday, May 15, at 3:48, eastern time, waving a sign
that read: *Obasanjo is a civilian dictator.*

The condition

of indigenous populations has to be clarified if postcolonial studies is to claim any kind of success. American Indians, making up the indigenous populations who have possessed this continent for thousands of years, claim a political status like no other population in the United States. Indians are not "minorities." They are not "people of color," vanishing or savage. Indians in America are citizens of indigenous nations who have been misnamed from the beginning of the colonization period. Indians possess a condition of dual citizenship that they have never surrendered; they possess dual citizenship as citizens of their native nations as well as the United States, ever since the United States conferred citizenship on them, in 1924. Indians are neither immigrants nor colonizers nor slaves nor tourists and, in the beginning, they were not Christians, either; had not been Christians for thousands of years before the missionaries came bringing with them the notion that they were welcome and essential. The thing to remember is that indigenous nations signed treaties with the United States and with other nations as well, namely France, England, Holland, indicating their sovereign status at first contact. Thus, succeeding generations have continued to claim native nation citizenship. This sets them apart from any other population in the United States, and confers upon them a political status unlike any other population in the United States.

It is one of the unfortunate realities of race dialogue in the United States that the enslavement of Africans for economic reasons and the belated effort to overthrow that crime against humanity have become the focus of contemporary dialogue and it can be called unfortunate for several reasons, among them: it implies that race issues are addressed only in black and white, that since the Civil War the failure of nationhood and sovereignty for Indians is off the table; it implies an end to racism is possible in the United States, an end to blackness and color coding is possible in the United States, that White America can overcome itself and its history of racism through knowledge, law, and intellectual endeavor.

I am not a believer in such redemption. It has been my observation that knowledge, law, and intellectual endeavor in the last couple of centuries have continued to deliberately misunderstand the condition of indigenous populations. It is obvious to anyone paying attention to studies in history and politics and race that from the early 1800s Indians have been colonized and America has been busy rationalizing that condition. Intellectually, postcolonial studies is a fraud, as the United States, now the only elephant in the jungle, is loathe to admit to its own history of enforced religiosity, colonialism, paternalism, and imperialism.

In order to remove ourselves from this dilemma, political difference must be the focus of interaction, not race or color or immigration or slavery.

There is the widespread notion

perpetuated on the television screen that if America had only had more "Arabic speakers" in its military and political structures, it would have been more successful in its invasion and occupation of Iraq (circa 2003). This is an idea that arises from the colonist rather than the nativist need and it is directly related to the notion of how the colonist can penetrate "the secrets" of the other. One is reminded of the Euroamerican-colonist based Christian ministers of the eighteenth and nineteenth century in America who learned the rudiments of native languages in order to subdue and convert the natives of this continent, make them forget their religions, and steal their lands.

I am always surprised at the presupposition that penetrating "the secrets" of the other through language is a moral and respectful thing to do. The question of how we understand others and how we understand ourselves is not just a question of war and peace; it is an academic question and it is an identity question and it is at the heart, perhaps, of what we can accept as intellectualism. "We only understand ourselves in conversations with others," said Rigoberta Menchu in her 1984 autobiography (p. 269) *I, Rigoberta Menchu ...* "with us, the Indians," she said. She was surveilled by skeptical scholars because she refused to answer certain queries, saying only that "Indians have secrets," suggesting that it is not always a good thing for these secrets to be revealed. She did not proffer intimacy and many were disappointed.

Dr. Robert Allen Warrior, in *Tribal Secrets,* wondered about the business of "secrets" when he speculated that the intellectualism of a people and its effects on the goals of the future (p. 123) are caught up in "a death dance of dependence between, on the one hand, abandoning ourselves to the intellectual strategies and categories of white, European thought and, on the other hand, declaring that we need nothing outside of ourselves and our cultures in order to understand the world and our place in it." It is a two-way street of responsibility. While such a position serves many possibilities, it does not get at the strategy that Menchu is accused of performing, what is called "a defensive move in the midst of her seduction."

While it is usually agreed that language is at the core of understanding and misunderstanding, especially in the alternative story told by natives, which may be one of the reasons for the effort to access "the other's" language, there is always the ambiguity in what it is the speakers/authors are trying to accomplish. What is the intent of those who wage war in the Arabian Peninsula and ask for speakers of Arab languages to come and help them? What was the intent of colonizers in early America who wanted to learn the languages of the natives? In the seductive Menchu case, it is easy to see what she knew about the role her native language might play in this, *the only indigenous account of genocide* on this continent *that has been recognized by the international community.* Even the murderous Indian "removal" policy in the United States, the subsequent theft of thousands of acres of land resulting in death and endemic poverty and disease, has not been called that. Genocide. Nor has it been recognized as that by the international community!!!

In the Summer

of 1851
for eighteen days
the tribes gathered at Fort Laramie

they feasted and smoked
and adopted one another's children
and declared peace
and gave "right-of-ways"
through their lands
opening up trade routes

non-tribal mail carriers fired upon them
and they fired back

from then on the Arapahoes
and the Sioux and the Cheyennes
were in a starving state

VI ✵✵✵

There are few vocations

like writing and the practice of poetry, for example, that are so uncalled for by the world . . . so unremunerative by any standards." William H. Gass, a philosopher and teacher who was born, by the way, in Fargo, North Dakota, wrote this in his insightful and wonderfully readable collection of essays called *Finding a Form*. I agree with him, but I have to wonder why this is so, when, in fact, I know so many writers who are delightful, esteemed, thoughtful, and serious.

Gass suggests that writers deserve better than indifference; but, do they?

Just as I was beginning to think there was no answer to this dilemma, I went to the South Dakota Festival of Books in Deadwood, South Dakota, on a warm, gorgeous day in October, 2003, and I began to reflect on why we who write and practice poetry are paid so little mind. It is because we often fail to say what we really know and think. We are, often, just too, too polite, which makes us too, too, wrong!!!

At the Deadwood Gulch Convention Center, it became clear to me that the world pays writers and historians so little mind because more often than not, we simply don't tell the truth. In my public utterances that day, I decided I'd go for it. I told my startled audience that this town, Deadwood, where so many writers were gathered on this day to tell their stories and read their poems, is an ugly town based in an ugly history and populated by an ugly people trying every day to rationalize their own ugly history of genocide and land theft. It is blatantly untrue, I said that day, that the "pioneers" and "settlers" and "gold diggers" who are the forefathers and foremothers of today's populations were not "invaders" and "murderers" and "thieves" of the sovereign lands of the Sioux. They were! Yet, neither that day, nor during the entire festival did I hear one story, one poem, one song that recognized the reality of historical theft and genocide that is at the heart of the town's history and present condition. Is it the denial of these realities that makes writers "uncalled for" in the larger sense that Gass speaks of?

Deadwood became a town, I told my audience that day, the same year that the Sioux killed Gen. George Armstrong Custer and his men when they invaded their Treaty Lands in 1876 for gold. It became a town as the U.S. Congress, in a fit of political revenge, passed the Black Hills Act of 1877, stealing 7.7 million acres, ignoring solemn pledges of Treaty. It was clear to me as I uttered those words that the invasion of another People's land, the subsequent theft and the killing off of thousands in the process of the takeover, cannot and should not be cause for creating the substance of a literary, artistic, spiritual heritage. We have found that only gold can do that. And, so, we are, yes, those of us who remember, uncalled for. Which means that no peaceful social landscape, so yearned for by all of us, can follow if denial or sheer ignorance is made credible by those who write. Historians and poets and writers have spent the last hundred years telling us lies: that the invasion by whites was a success, the battlefield victory of the Indians was not, and the future is for those who claim it whichever way they can. Why would we poets, and historians who write and practice poetry, be taken seriously if what is known of the subject we are writing about is so badly attended? One can only think of the killings at Macondo in Garcia Marquez's *One Hundred Years of Solitude*, which tells us about the massacre . . . that never happened.

I was the only poet that day who spoke on these matters.

It is sad to say that these fields of barren history will produce no Garcia Marquez.

The Way It Is
1990

Living here
in the hills, walking
a predestined path
at the edge of swiftwater,
the sound of the wind exchanges stories
with birds chatting of good harvest

they say:
hwo come, sing to remember
wacipo come, dance to forget

all the rituals sound the same
as when our ancestors smoked
the inner bark of red willow

landmarks here of the prairie wildflowers
pay their latest respects as the chilly fall air
catches white coils from the cigarette
I shelter behind the breeze.
October passes, good times and memories
recede with the wind.

Colonization

Were I a painter
I, too, would paint
history by denial

to prove the point
that oil and tone
and color and design
are part of the tragic problem.

Trying to Make a Difference

Hanging on the breeze
touching but not touching
a yellow jacket hovers in the eaves
dizzy in the hot sun
unable to hear any music but his own

he slips into my glass of sweet tea
drawn by the amber, the bouquet, the honey
giving in to his own lust, he struggles
for his life

with the tip of my thumbnail
I end it.

Rabbit Dance

> (a brother told me this before he didn't come back
> from the war)

Off the coast of Pusan
he thought of a woman and the childhood
which had never left his memory: like a white moth
flapping skyward in early November, taking wrong signals
he got his pay and went on liberty riding the buses
to the courtyards and curved bridges.

Tiole! Tiole!
he wanted the Korean girls to look at him
and invite him home

and they did.

At the last minute he wanted
to speak as men of the prairie do
to sing the *mastincina* songs
remember the silent grace
of her shawl about him

to come home
and dance with her again.

Korea 1952

December Twenty-Eight

wa 'hde ca pi (What Women Say)

Gray comes after the holiday
shading my voice at the river bank
it dulls the tinsel
swaying
from plucked tree limbs

inside, bits of bark crackle
in warm embers and the white cat curls
roundly beside the darkened door

my gaze seeks out the fog in the distance
as it mists the mountain tops

at rest, I have no explanation
for the tears
that fill my eyes

Sitting Beside an American Woman on an International Flight Leaving Seattle Heading for the Crow Creek
1973

Teheran is an ugly city
    my husband is now in Egypt
    works in the oil industry

They have no toys for their children
    they love their children
    my friend looked in all their museums
    I don't know why
    they have no toys for their children
    they love their children
But, probably because they were nomadic
    they have no toys for their children

Place the mask over your nose
and breathe deeply

They have no history
    beyond the Koran,
    you know.
they can't possibly run the oil fields
    they have no knowledge
we have blackouts constantly
    in Egypt
the poor   the poor   the poor

Place the mask over your nose
and breathe deeply

We go in and dig the wells
    and plant the trees
    everything
then we go somewhere else
    and do the same
we've been everywhere
Texas
Oklahoma
Alaska
Iran
Afghanistan
and now Egypt

He called and said
    surreptitiously
    we are to go to Moscow
    and Leningrad

my servants say
    I leave them no dignity
    I don't know what they mean

I try
so hard
to help
what I used to give them, I now say,

"You must pay
even a little ...
for it."

Place the mask over your nose
And breathe deeply

Soft drinks?
you want a beer?
smoking? non-smoking?

Yea. . . . place the mask. . . .

I see pastel greens and yellows
against jelly bean windows
disturbing the silver flash of wings

the white blue sky

hovers.

Out of the Mouths of Babes

"Who will tell the stories?" is an essay I wrote years ago. The question suggests that stories are as important as poetry. If they are the major source for poems, as some would believe, they, too, deserve recitation.

Libelous and hardcore ignorance rising out of unavoidable historical neurosis is hard for Indians to face up to, but when it emerges in childish, elemental, primitive behavior of the innocent, we know we cannot turn back the clock, we cannot press charges; we know that, in the larger sense, wounds endure and permanent scars are what they are for all of us, both whites and Indians. And so, we remember the story:

"Are you with your family?"

Her flushed, tense face was suddenly only inches from mine, a desperation in her eyes, her wispy, thin bangs damp with perspiration. She stood in the aisle, the only person on the entire aircraft swathed in wool and nylon meant for the ski slopes.

"Uh ... no," I looked up from my books and glanced at the two black military men who shared my space. They looked straight ahead.

"Well ...," said in a girlish voice, crisp and self-confident, "would you mind, then, sitting back here?"

Pause.

"... so my kids can sit up here?"

Another pause.

"Then I can sit here between my husband, here, and him, our

friend." She gestured first to the children, then to the men in her entourage, pointing to a young man already seated beside another youthful man in the process of taking off a red and blue ski jacket.

"Then I can watch them," she went on looking at the little girls "...up here.... see.... in front of me, instead of there across the aisle."

She put one manicured hand on the back of my chair and with the other pointed to the two little girls, about nine and ten years of age already seated across the aisle from me and forward. Their seat belts were buckled and they sat quietly.

My briefcase was already open, my lap full of papers.

"Well," I said, hesitating. Then I decided to assert myself honestly. "Well, no." Smiling. "I'd rather not."

She stood still, disappointment and accusation and disbelief in her frenzied eyes "Oh?" She looked back at her husband, eyes darkening. I looked up at her with what I thought was an air of apology.

"Oh ... well then," she said loudly, her face moving close to mine. "You'll understand, then, won't you, when they behave obnoxiously!" Her breath smelled like peppermint. Her hands flitted around her streaming hair. Her tongue hissed the words. She turned quickly and went down the aisle of the aircraft apparently looking for a stewardess. A few moments later she returned and sat down between the two men who sat passively, one on each side of her.

Soon the stewardess came over and asked the two young black servicemen sitting next to me to exchange places with the children across the aisle. They obediently reached for their carry-on cases and politely settled themselves in the forward seats. Then the two little white-haired girls crawled over me and my papers into the vacated seats. They fastened their seat belts.

Their mother, seated between the two men behind us, hissed instructions: "Brandy," she called. When the little girl turned, the mother held her nose, filled her lungs with air, and built pressure in her ears as the plane lifted into the air.

The child, looking scared, performed the apparently pre-rehearsed action to assure herself and her mother that things would work out well and no undue ear problems would be the result of this flight.

"Sit down now," the mother hissed redundantly to the securely seated children.

"Fasten your seat belt again," she instructed in a loud, angry voice. The little girls settled back. I went back to my papers.

"Junie," the mother whispered loudly at our shoulders. The littlest girl, near the window, cocked her head around her sister trying to look at her mother.

"Do you have to go potty?"

"Yes!" the child responded eagerly.

"Me, too!" shouted Brandy.

They climbed over knees, purse, papers as they made their way to the aisle.

"Return to your seats," the stewardess instructed coming from the opposite direction as the "FASTEN YOUR SEAT BELTS" sign came on abruptly and we hit unexpected turbulence.

The trio returned from their uncompleted trip to the "potty," again plunging over knees and shoe tops.

"Just sit!" the mother instructed hoarsely.

I looked back at her. She smiled showing her perfectly white teeth. She spread her lovely hands, palms upward.

As I put my book down, closed my eyes and waited, the plane climbed above the wind stream.

When the plane settled into its pattern, the pilot's reassuring voice came on the intercom with a plausible apology. Potty was forgotten by those seated near me.

In a few moments, the blessed silence was broken:

"Are you a Indian," asked Junie.

"Yes."

"I knew it!!" she exclaimed triumphantly. "You're wearing turquoise!"

"Are you a squaw?" she persisted, drawing out the last syllable of the offensive word.

"Uh . . . m . . ."

She looked up earnestly waiting for my answer. Blue-eyes. Innocent.

"U-mm-m—No," I said at last.

She wrinkled her brow.

"You're no-oo-o-t?"

She flopped back in her seat and pursed her mouth in disgust.

Clearly, her disappointment in me was palpable.

In spite of my obvious failure to please, I turned away and so did the little girl. Nothing wrong here, I thought in the interest of my usual need to pretend such libelous and hard-core ignorance didn't matter. Just an unavoidable historical neurosis, oh yeah?

I slept all the way to Denver and so did my seat companions.

A Cynic Assumes the Right to Be Morally Irresponsible Near the Grand River

1993

Witnessing the way of life of men
who pull buffalo skulls in dusty prairie arbors

we are relatives in the old way
yet, we keep one eye on the door

trying for the cosmopolitan language
of the world at large stealing away at dusk
with the jazz players to a crowded room
across from the Minneapolis Art Institute

preferring our own company
we do not speak of stories in debt to
predecessors ever-present
and real

in this paradox lie
deep meanings
that might have been useful

a hundred years ago.

Restless Spirit

the sun drops below the horizon
darkening shadows on every bush

I'm thinking of your absences
how and why you come and go

even now, while elsewhere,
you rouse the lifting embers
of my flaming need to know
how and why you come and go

amidst my agitation, the quail arrive en masse
and take your place in my thoughts for a moment

settling into unlit grassy slopes
of greasewood above the
little house we share

they hide in hillsides
then swarm into the sky again
sudden crowds of them
humming
clustering around

tempting secrets about how and why
you come and go

are carried off by the wind
and by you ringleader, provocateur,
troublemaker
arsonist

Culture Wars

1988

Slave badges from Charleston
sell now for 4,000 dollars
Lakota shirts are so priceless
even Indians fail to mourn the dead.

fatally flawed, mildly surprised by
revolutionary gestures of a century ago,
the young and the restless let go of Memory's
struggle against forgetting: they make
money imagining a contradictory past.

Milan Kundera, having faced
the Russian tanks
could tell them a thing or two: *"man
has always wanted to wipe out the tracks,
both his own and others."*

While Watching a Prairie Bird
1998

I,
escapee from lecture rooms,
soft hands and red pencils,
stand still
watching a ruffled grouse
in the silence
of an overcast Columbia River
afternoon.

I,
dropout from the pristine Ivory Tower,
walk again the forest fringe,
glimpse a bird through limbs
of yellowed aspen leaves, see
cautious stepping, long pauses,
ruffling neck feathers and
snapping head movements

the fantail spreading

about to vanish into
the dead, browned brush of November

careful
watchful

I hear the muffled thunder sounds
of the gray grouse's hidden
territorial defense

and know the sounds are mine.

VII ❧ ❧ ❧

Great literary events

are in the offing if Leonard Peltier ever gets out of jail. That is the only opinion I have on the decades-long case concerning the American Indian Movement's most celebrated prisoner. Either he shot those officers or he didn't. We don't know. What we do know is that he probably did not get a fair trial. His public appearances concerning these matters if and when he is released will go on endlessly just as the political dialogue concerning his guilt or innocence has been interminable. This is a civil rights case, not a treaty rights case. The issue of a fair trial in the American judicial system is an individual rights issue. These are the kinds of cases that do two things: (1) they either bring about bad law for Indian nations, or, if we are lucky (2) they become meaningless to Tribal Nationhood and we move on.

Phyllis Schlafly says this:

"Many years ago Christian pioneers had to fight savage Indians. Today, missionaries of these former cultures are being sent via the public schools to heathenize our children."

It continues to be difficult for me to come to grips with the hatred that others feel toward us, our histories, our cultures. We in Indian Studies like to think that we are not atheists, that we are, instead, thoughtful people intent upon developing an *ethno-endogenous epistemological model* of education in the United States, and we would like to think that what we are doing is long overdue. The issue here, for me, is not how to bridge the gap between Christians and the indigenous history of this country because it is apparently an unbridgeable gap. It might be best to simply acknowledge it and go about the work in defensive and transformative education and politics, about which I care deeply.

The Sioux say,

"We were once the star people." There was nothing but water everywhere, the story goes, and darkness; and the wind was our only relative. The wicun appeared but they would not give out much light because the moon would do that. And they would not give out much heat because the sun would do that. And, so, the Dakotahs, who were lost in the universe, were helped into humanity by the wicun, who placed them in the skies of the Northern Plains. They became the Dakota, Lakota, and Nakota, recognized by the spirits in the Paha Sapa and the places the red and black pipestone makes holy. The star people were given language and so, they say, too, that language is sacred. We are called now Ikce Wicasta.

The Morning World Is Like This

All people begin as the stars begin,
leaning toward the pungent earth
waiting for the sun. Time moves them
to the damp waterline and then
crimson bulbs of knowledge
burst like comets in the fading darkness of morning.

Ta te, the wind, ages in earthly daytime,
rattling windows, lifting skirts
like a ruthless annoyance
remembered as older than the earth's
first season.

It wakes me early
and the geese are already in the
November sky, strutting in
elegant secrecy, faint in their
cries for perfect procession.
Where do they go? What will become of them?

I am waking and I have nothing to do
but wait for the sun.

November 19, 2005

This afternoon I stood amongst the Indian books on the second floor
of the Black Hills Prairie Edge Bookstore and listened to people from
this rugged western town and its adjoining Indian Reservations say
"goodbye" to the preeminent Sioux scholar Vine Deloria Jr., dead at
72. There has been only a handful of scholars in my lifetime who have
changed the ways that Indians think of themselves after years of being
told we were "defeated" and "vanished." Vine was one of them who
challenged the anthropologists' talk of our Indian-white histories in
America as merely the unfortunate "clash of cultures," with Indians
not long for this world and, alas, no hand to be identified as criminal.
Vine was the one who introduced Indians to the political language of
genocide, theft, paternalism, invasion, and colonialism . . . a language
we immediately recognized as our own.

Raised and educated in places other than Harvard and Yale,
Deloria spent his career exposing what America has wanted to think
of itself and in the process gave us the vision to defend ourselves. He
came along in the 1960s and '70s, that time when Red Crow tells us
"we came close to the end."

This afternoon, there was much sadness and we thumbed through
the dozens of books he wrote throughout the years. Yet, there were a lot
of jokes, too, told in remembrance of this remarkable man's legendary
sense of humor, which he inherited from his father . . . and, lots of tears
from people who told how much he meant to them.

Gerald One Feather, an old *Sicangu kola* from Rosebud, said a
prayer in Lakota, a language Vine never knew, asking us to remember
this good man he called Ikce Wicasta.

I said a few words, telling one of Vine's "relocation" jokes about "standing at the corner of walk and don't walk." You remember that one? It is a tired old Indian joke, but everyone laughed, grateful for the moment.

We lingered in the cozy bookstore, reluctant to leave as we all asked the unanswerable question: "Why must good men die too soon?"

Must We Go to Delphi...?

Today's idea about Democracy is that if America is to fulfill its destiny it must do so with a certain kind of missionary and/or fundamentalist zeal. That is not a new idea in America but one I've always found to be self-righteous and extreme. Nowadays, such ideas make me hostile to the notion that religion can have any role at all in Government. This hostility in me has become more textured and easier to digest since the 2002 and 2004 elections and 9/11. Now I will come right out and say it: I am against religion in government. I'm with Voltaire these days, who said it is necessary to "wipe out that rubbish," that is, religion.

This has not been easy for me to say, since I know that American Indians at large have been saying that nothing is secular, not government, not society, not war, not death; that "spirituality" is in everything and it is everywhere. All Indian gatherings in Sioux Country, without exception, begin with a prayer. At every *wacipi,* just following the "grand entry," the old guys get up to the microphone and begin: "*Ate oyape mahpiya kté....*" and the dancers wiggle on one foot, then the other, children dash between the chairs and the drum, old women clutch their shawls, and teenagers stroll out in the aisles munching fries. Yes, prayer presents a ceremonial beginning to anything, school programs, tribal council meetings, feasts, and basketball; like the great festivals of ancient Greece in the name of Apollo referencing the oracle at Delphi....

This behavior on the part of Indians seems to fit right in with the recent mainstream effort in America to "restore God" to government. It is a terrible idea. It is a contradiction that anyone who knows history finds beyond hypocritical. No one in America defended the

Indian right to God when the early IRA governments were formed in 1934. Even today, no one in America defends the Muslim right to God in the "new" governments of Iraq or Egypt. The hypocrisy is that America does not respect other religions and, in fact, thinks democratic institutions can survive ONLY IF SECULAR GOVERNMENT IS EMBEDDED IN CHRISTIAN FAITH. In fact, America has struggled for two hundred years to stamp out all religious figures except Christ. To talk, then, of religion in government is not only an awful idea, it is false piety at its zenith, unworkable and meaningless.

Governments can be democratic, sane, organized, and humane without god only if church and state do not confuse themselves, and people remain responsible to one another. American Indians in the old days untangled the state from the clergy, traditionally speaking, and it was only after they became Christians that they began the argument. This is not to say that societies must or must not be ruled by science, knowledge, and civilization. What must rule them is their tribal trust in one another.

Dakota Iapi Tewahi(n)da

is a native Sisseton song
I heard in a gray, drafty gymnasium
some years ago. Hearing it for the first time

made me sad because all the old speakers
are gone now: they, who could not write their
American names and did not speak English

a guitar player, during the break, says
we have "40 miles to go"

when Joe's wife waves at me
I begin to know we are acknowledging
our separate grief   men sing at the drum, frightened
of each age, now theirs, whose task it is to remember
she listens and hugs her sleepy grandson

but the guitar player says:
something happens in the new song
telling of murdered Indians
all of the epics of heroism
to amaze ourselves

I hold my breath
and know that when I am really old, I will
live alone, without husband,
without child, requiring
nothing but the song.

There is a man

we all know, an Oglala Lakota, who has been successfully growing hemp crops on his lands on the Oglala Sioux Reservation in western South Dakota for several years only to have those crops consistently destroyed by federal agents after every growing season. His contracts with other hemp growers in Canada have been unmet and his hemp operation is in dire straits financially speaking.

It may be time for federal and state laws to be rewritten concerning the growing of industrial hemp crops, in the same manner that other laws have been rewritten as social movements and progress toward better understanding has occurred. For example, the S.D. Code of laws in 1919, which said that Indians and whites could not enter into marriage contracts or cohabit as husband and wife, was repealed on March 3, 1925, simply because state laws and federal control conflicted in the opinions and, more to the point, the law was simply unworkable, racist, and repressive. The state and federal laws forbidding the growth and possession of Indian hemp (described then as cannabis, Indian or cannabis sativa, commonly known as Indian hemp, hashish, or marijuana in its raw state) was approved by HB 326 March 6, 1931, and was based, largely, on faulty information concerning industrial hemp and its relationship to marijuana. These laws, too, are unworkable and repressive.

In 1923, about the time Indians were granted U.S. citizenship, the state of South Dakota had argued successfully against the growth of hemp, not on the basis that it wasn't a legitimate industrial crop, but, rather, on the basis that it was dangerous and laws were needed to preserve health, to preserve public peace, health, and safety. As we all know, industrial hemp is not a "stupefying drug," and needs no more regulation than the state puts on cheese and butter. Hemp is not an "exhilarating drug" that needs to be regulated; thus, state and federal laws must change. The idea that in 1923, state and federal laws prohibited the possession and sale of peyote or mescal has, also, taken a new turn, since religious use of it has been recognized, but, that argument has little or nothing to do with growing industrial hemp as an economic development on the lands possessed for ages by the Sioux Tribe. Religion and economics are two different things, I would posit. It is time for the federal government (and its complicit state governments) to grow up, and relinquish its colonial control of Indian lands in the matter of producing industrial hemp.

Metaphor
A 1990s Café Stalled in the Vapor Lock of History

On the streets of the town where I live in the Black Hills of South Dakota there is a sweet café that could be any café in any town. But it's not just any café in any town. It's in the "hills," after all, and it is called the McGillycuddy Café, and it is located on quiet streets that lead eventually to the Shrine of Democracy, south of this town.

You can get a foamy latte in this café, a strawberry sweet roll slathered with creamy butter, and you can settle down to read the volumes of a marvelous collection of fiction, nonfiction, and poetry in one of the best privately owned bookstores for miles around. Comfortable chairs fill the rooms and soft carpets cover the floors of the two levels of the shop. The outside patio filled with sun and fragrant flowers is irresistible.

Once when I was driving down this street in the summer heat, my uncle's car vapor locked, and I was stalled. Had to get help. Make a phone call. I went into the café, not noticing its name, and was treated with the casual kindness that people are known for around here. Didn't even charge me the quarter. Those of you who drive Indian cars know what I mean about vapor lock; that's when the gasoline liquid turns to a vapor, gets hot in the gas line, too close to the manifold; the gas forms and blocks the liquid and the car starves for gasoline. The gas can't go into the carburetor and the engine starves and stalls. You gotta wait until the gas cools inside the line. Or maybe make a phone call. Maybe you can use a wet rag to wrap the line, but, that's only if you are 50 miles from anywhere, like when you are driving on the rez.

I looked around the café that day, smiling, until my eyes fell upon the sign above the door. **McGillycuddy Café.** Oh-Ho . . . this is a café, I thought then, with a name vapor locked in historical conflict, a café trying to cool a red-hot passionate history that can't be cooled. It'll take more than a phone call or time or the wrapping of a wet rag, I mused. This is a café that holds in its name a seat of honor for a man who found a place among the dozens of cunning, brilliant, and ruthless bureaucrats who ran the colonial institutions of government on Indian Reservations in this country in years gone by, a man whose name was and is known by everybody, a man who was overseer to racism and genocide in a democracy often portrayed as one of the greatest experiments in government known to mankind.

But it was never that.

McGillycuddy's honor took shape during the hot summertime of genocide, though no one in the café admits to this reality. Many of the tales told by Midwestern whites about the period from 1850–1890, when McGillycuddy lived, are based in tellings that deny and excuse blood feuds, racism, colonial politics, genocide, and land theft. They are pure fiction and outright lies that have poisoned the lines to the carburetor of Indian-white dialogue in this town for a hundred years. The events of the past, unattended for many decades, seem too close to the manifold of realism, overheated. Stalled.

The café and its name are based in the notion that Indian Agent Dr. Valentine T. McGillycuddy can be claimed as a virtuous historical figure in Western South Dakota. It is based in a fiction and a lie intended to say that the war against Sioux treaty rights marked by the fingerprints of men like McGillycuddy is an honorable history. It is intended to say that those who profited from those years of death and poverty are deserving of our praise.

The truth is, McGillycuddy was an essential cog in an anti-Indian machine directed toward killing off Indians as a race of people, which was the policy of the time. If you don't believe it, I refer you to the writings of the 1868 second session of the 40th Congress of the United States, which explored extermination or Reservation policy, both in conflict with the treaty rights and human rights of the Sioux tribes. Agent McGillycuddy was part and parcel of the Christian and local political communities of that era reflected in a national policy that hated and feared Indians, held them in great contempt, and forced upon them landlessness, poverty, and disease. Unfortunately, for the three centuries that have followed the early Indian Reservation Era of which McGillycuddy was an essential cog, hatred and fear and contempt have driven forward motifs and tellings that have now become the contrived yet acceptable history of the period; the attempt to glorify McGillycuddy is a major thrust of that history. Thus, we community survivors, both white and Indian, sit among the ruins of history, among the stunning collection of books and the sun and the flowers. We sit, sip a tasty latte while waiting for the auto parts man, and many of us know that some of the stories we hear and tell are very troubling, some are tragic, and all of them are scandalous.

The motifs of the anti-Indian historiography McGillycuddy was a part of can quickly be described as follows: Indians killed whites indiscriminately because they were savages, Indians tortured whites and stole their children because they were barbarians, Indians have always been a timeless menace that must be wiped out completely, Indians are pitiful remnants of a doomed race, and whites in leadership positions of that era and all those following periods are known to have acted virtuously and patriotically and humanely in the face of an unassimilable population of indigenous societies who claimed to be the landowners. Finally, whites have the right to the land and its resources. Indians do not.

With nothing more than anti-Indianism (hatred and fear and contempt of Indians) at the heart of historical and present-day white imagination, regional historians have fashioned a whole story: In the first years of the new century of 2000, the McGillycuddy Speaker Series is initiated at the university he helped found a hundred years ago, the South Dakota School of Mines and Technology in Rapid City, South Dakota. Originally this institution was founded to assist in the legalization of land theft, and, to extract the minerals of the region and, more recently, it has become renowned in order to reinvent the most hated Indian Agent of any time and any place, Dr. Valentine T. McGillycuddy, U.S. Federal Agent of the Oglala Sioux at Pine Ridge from the war and Reservation period of the 1860s to the 1890s, as a heroic and virtuous historical figure. This history is serving the colonial takeover of a vast region by unscrupulous means. It is outright historical lying.

The period in question does not deserve to be whitewashed by local image makers as a period of legal treat with Indians. Indeed, historians of all stripes and, particularly, the historian Helen Hunt Jackson, have called these years in American History the "century of dishonor." There can be no doubt that following the treaty making period, the McGillycuddy regime at Pine Ridge Reservation was responsible for a virulent anti-Indianism in law and society that continues to this day. McGillycuddy, himself, was no mere bystander, and for his participation in the genocidal practices of the era, he ended up an argumentative overseer who had many conflicts with just about everyone he met and as one of the richest men in the region, a university president, a writer of the state constitution, and the initiator of a Reservation-based government modeled in the U.S. theory of colonization whose manmade historical forces converged into a murderous genocidal policy. This policy continued until the middle of the twentieth century when a Reorganization period ensued.

During the McGillycuddy years, Indian leaders were assassinated, an occupational police force was settled on all of the Indian homelands, U.S. Armies roamed the countryside killing natives at will, spiteful and self-serving stories by whites born of racist theories harbored for generations were raised to the stature of Historiography, and dozens of laws were passed to disenfranchise natives. At a time when native peoples had no access to the U.S. court systems, Crazy Horse and Sitting Bull and hundreds of other leaders were assassinated by federal troops; the Major Crimes Act went into effect, eliminating traditional native law and order structures, causing endemic chaos; the Allotment Act was passed in violation of treaty rights, bringing a loss of land and economic survival; native children were stolen from their homes and sent to boarding schools, sometimes never to return. A disturbingly large number of people in the Midwest now believe that Indians, made homeless and poverty-stricken by these policies, are simply to accept their fate and accept McGillycuddy, not as an anti-Indian bureaucrat, but as a hero of the people and the West. The raising of McGillycuddy to heroic status assists in whitewashing this awful history because he was one of the centerpieces to the success of this attempt at genocide.

There can be no greater crime than to force a delusional version of white/colonial history on the schoolchildren of this region, both Indian and white. Thoughtful people must reject this revisionist history and, instead, describe such figures as McGillycuddy within the framework of a genocidal, racist federal policy, as a powerful figure who by his actions and his inactions oversaw the killing of Indians and the theft of a continent. If no one writes or speaks to the shamefulness of this refashioning of McGillycuddy as a heroic figure, the treachery, deception, bribery, and assassination tools of such history will be expanded like gas in the manifold, and an unparalleled moment in Indian-white relations will be forever fraudulent. Overheated. Stalled. Blocking the fluid of truth and reason.

As America faces another colonial war, this time in the Middle East, the question of how this fraudulent history just described is to be played out on the world stage as this nation, just a few centuries old, achieves its place in the future must be asked by every historian and writer and grandmother and poet of our time. It must be asked as we sit in comfort in the McGillycuddy Café on our way to the Shrine of Democracy. Phone calls? Wet rags around the hot lines? Time? What will it take for the Indian world and the non-Indian world to start the engine, shift gears, and move on down a new road?

Anangoptan (Listen!)

If we are defining war crimes,
I am listening

I am listening!

when I hear young men talk
I worry that they may be persuaded
to go to war

from 1961 to 1969,
    before they were born
another generation of young men
was persuaded to do
chemical warfare bombing
in places called South and North Vietnam

what has become of them?

before they were born
before they were born

I listen
they are talking

they know nothing of the Nuremberg Trials
which took place
    before they were born

before they were born
before they were born

    what it said
    and what it meant

it said:
if we are defining war crimes,
the supreme crime is aggression

if we are defining war crimes
the supreme crime is aggression
the supreme crime is aggression

are they listening?

Make Believe

> ...in the first decade of 2k, native actors of stunning
> excellence play out the stylish multicolored fiesta....

(a poem for Graham Greene and Wes Studi)

about the ways you take part in the redemptive myth,
the new television Western story,
I say this:

there is nothing redemptive
about coming to a place uninvited
and stealing other people's land, killing
thousands of innocent people
and passing laws that make them
persona non grata in the dissolution
of their own homelands

and there is nothing heroic
about participating
in the disturbing betrayal and violation
of sumptuous, intense suicide

it's just idle talk
nothing that should
engender
nationalistic
pride

the history of America, they say,
fosters something to be remembered:
the leaf lifted by the wind to resurrection
or the horse and the gun

   You are to meditate
on the masterpieces of the white man
since all of the Sioux heroes have been murdered

and the scriptwriters,
devotional and philosophic,
awake us all to the noise of the crowd.

New Myths of Feminism

Indian people
have not forgiven
Sacajawea

she disappears
from the tribal story,
the furthest sorrow

She's now given to literary composition,
films, and Lewis and Clark diaries
in solemn moments of pure color
to expose, to utter, to recite
the white man's enormous
vision expressing
native ruins

What is a feminist?

I'm called a feminist sometimes, but I don't know exactly what
that means. Here in the West, we are told the first feminist was
Annie Oakley, who could shoot a dime out of a man's thumb and
forefinger at a hundred yards. Others think the first feminist was
Mary Wollstonecraft, who in 1792 crossed the English channel to
Revolutionary France just, one supposes, to be near danger and show
no fear. She was a writer, of course, which makes her much more
interesting to me than if she were a sharpshooter. One of her first
publications was *A Vindication of the Rights of Woman* and later she
published *A Vindication of the Rights of Men.*

She gave birth to a daughter, Mary Shelley, who wrote *Frankenstein,*
and became almost immortal to publishers and movie makers
throughout the world. An aside: this could mean, I suppose, that
becoming a writer is in the blood. Who believes that? Art talent is
inherited? What would Woody say about Arlo?

But what Wollstonecraft did that makes her a feminist in the eyes
of the literati is this: she not only wrote books, she wrote reviews of
books at a time when most books were written by men. She became
a professional reviewer, a profession that takes guts even now, to say
nothing of how precarious it must have been in her time, when taking
part in the controversies of literary life was almost never a part of a
woman's life. Certainly, in her time and ours, a woman's voice has not
been an acceptable part of political commentary, which has almost
always been thought of as a male preserve. Reviewing books takes
great courage, as well as a decent vocabulary. It is a challenge. For Mary
Wollstonecraft feminism drove her to write and assess the works of

others. For me, Indianism (some call it Indigenism) is what moves me, and I want to call myself not a feminist, but rather, an Indianist in the writing world.

Reviewing books could become a passion of mine, if only I had more time, not because I want to be a feminist, nor because I want to break new ground, but, because, as Wollstonecraft wanted to invent feminist thinking that might rid the world of male oppression, I want to invent Indianist thinking to appraise those works that assume primacy concerning the lives of American Indians, most of it written by white males, but some these days by white female wannabees. Reviewing books is an activity that gives an outsider these days the right to a point of view in an ever-expanding and continuing white-male and anti-Indian industry. I would have liked to have taken book reviewing seriously at some earlier point in my career, and I would like to have achieved as a writer an appropriate description of myself in doing so.

Often, book reviewers are called all sorts of unkind names not only by historians but, also, by people who are on the same page. H. L. Mencken is a good example. There were all sorts of people who didn't speak to him throughout the years as they read his political and literary critiques. One longtime colleague even threatened a lawsuit. Reviewers with strong opinions must just get used to it. The kindest thing that was said about me recently was that I was a "doyenne" in Indian Studies, which means, I think, that I am an old woman, and who can argue with that? Just recently, a friend sent me an essay called "Why I Can't Read Elizabeth Cook-Lynn," by one Jackson J. Benson, published in *Down by the Lemonade Springs: Essays on Wallace Stegner* (University of Nevada Press, 2001). Benson's redundant title lacks originality as one immediately recognizes the takeoff on my 1996 collection of essays, *Why I Can't Read Wallace Stegner and Other Essays: A Tribal Voice* (University of Wisconsin Press), in which I say Stegner's influence in creating the Western Myth omits Indians except as they are pitiful and vanished. Benson says I am very, very angry, hard-hearted, unaware, and not well read in the Stegner oeuvre, hateful, self-righteous, wrong, and simplistic.

In response to that I say I hold no grudges. But, more to the point, it seems to me that literary discussions are the most exciting discussions around ... even more fun than the political or psychological or historical or legal discussions I ordinarily go for; and it seems to me, too, that we don't need to call each other names in the process of "airing the dirty laundry," which is what Ishmael Reed calls this kind of discourse.

There is much disagreement, of course, about the business of writing reviews. My friend who teaches in Michigan tells me, "Liz, I only write reviews of books I LIKE."

"Well, then, you are not a feminist, are you?"

"No, of course not," he replied, laughing.

"Nor are you an Indianist!"

"No," he said, in all seriousness. "I'm an intellectual!!!"

I lifted my eyebrows and fell into an immediate silence.

Since most of us in Indian Studies don't appear on television, since our work is not seen in the *New York Review of Books* and we aren't often asked to speak out on public issues, since we rarely write screenplays and since most of us were not the founders of AIM, how is it, then, that we are to be heard? Do we even have a responsibility to be heard outside of our immediate enclaves? Is it our "thing," to assault and interrogate ideas? Or is that notion of failed responsibility to other communities, both academic and rural, just a tribal code that can be easily dismissed? What do we do in the course of academic Indian Studies? It is my view that what we have seen when we forced criticism to change directions starting, perhaps, with Vine Deloria's *Custer Died for Your Sins*, was a movement miles away from the anthropologist's "clash of culture" mode of assessment, and even farther away from the "feminist's" call for inclusion as we assert ourselves into an entirely new epistemology. We may not be there, yet, but we are on our way!

I am convinced that there are distinctive "indigenist" ways of knowing. This is a theory that probably cannot be born out scientifically, but it is a conviction born of sensory and introspective experience. Moreover it is a conviction brought about because of the particular political nature of the indigenous-colonial paradigm that is inescapable for anyone who has lived as an Indian in America. Cultural norms, also, which rise out of the long tenure of tribal peoples in specific places that most of us revere, have a lot to do with it. If Eurocentrism is a way of knowing, and some believe it is, then saying that there is an indigenist way of knowing can, also, be a real thing, not just a way to blame historians or subjugation or victimization, but, rather, a way to negotiate the world that is more than intuition, even more than reason.

Sometimes it seems so simple, yet when we try to recall specific experiences that might defend the idea of indigenist ways of knowing, we are called anti-intellectual, thinking with the heart, not the head. Several years ago I attended a conference on "feminism" at the University of Minnesota where a male singer/dancer of the Sicangu Tribe of Indians from South Dakota was booed off the stage as he introduced female participants in a dance performance and as he sang for their presentations. "Let them speak for themselves," the feminists shouted. It was shocking to hear three thousand mostly white female academics, members of the National Women's Studies association, hiss and boo, collectively condemning a man revered in his tribal community, a man who ended up trying to defend himself from this outrage by pleading, *"I am a good man. The People think I am a good man, and I have come here at the invitation of my relatives."* He gestured toward the female dancers, who stood transfixed. This story is not told here to condemn "feminism," because, who knows? This experience may have been an anomaly in Women's Studies spheres. I can't say, because I've not attended a Women's Studies event since.

Ideally, the possibility that there is such a thing as an indigenist way of knowing is treated with some respect in many situations and that is what was expected by this group of American Indians at this unfortunate meeting. The churlish behavior of white "feminists" was stunning in its ignorance of the belief that the relationship between male and female is a precious thing in the Sicangu Lakota way of thinking, as it is in all tribal, indigenous cultures, not just a matter of dominance and submission. It is a mythic, psychological, spiritual matter that stems not from academic research but from an indigenous worldview that connects not only the sexes but, also, elements and species of the universe in familial and humanistic ways. It is expressed communally in the dance, in the song.

If that is the case, critics say, why is it then that "domestic violence," that is, the expression of hatred, anger, and oppression toward women by men, is a major problem in Indian communities? Why is it that a study by the *Christian Science Monitor* (October 12, 1990) tells us that every fifteen seconds an American woman is abused by her partner and it is no different for an American Indian woman? The answers to that question are complex, but surely we must recognize that ideals are almost always separate from reality in human life. A society may have ideal ways of looking at the world, yet violate those ways in everyday human existence. History is replete with evidence for that possibility.

In any event, feminist studies and American Indian Studies have become important movements toward the ever-expanding epistemologies of the academic world. As Wollstonecraft wanted to invent feminist thinking, she also wanted to deflate the pretensions of male dominance. So, too, do Indianist scholars want to investigate falsehoods about them and expose the fraud and propaganda that sometimes pass for scholarship.

Snowy Days and Nights

    unlike those rainy Sunday afternoons
    of April in front of television sets
are best spent in the kitchen
to begin measuring gray skies
only to discover
you are
out of cinnamon
that tropical Asian aromatic bark
that comes from the sweet, warm hands
of princes, rulers, and captains.

Drying rubber overshoes
leak their grim clumps on the glossy deck,
bare branches hang against the dim sky.
Huge yellow plows scrape over paved crusts
in the distance and gleaming lights
spot deer and mountain sheep
scurrying for cover.

I knead the soft, thick dough
sprinkling in the substitute cloves
and nutmeg. . . .
I fry it in deep fat and
watch the fog close in.

Rejoice, Rejoice

At church gatherings
we sat with white folks
whose generous, servile, smelling of blue soap
children gave us brown sacks of moldy fruit
because we were needy Indians
no longer landlords. Dispossessed
by the generous and servile fruit givers,
we sat behind inaudible ghosts
of historical betrayal.

Our silences on those Sundays
rang in cloistered ears
while swells of sound rose round:
I Serve Thee, Jesus.

Below the Poverty Line

There are many days in December that reach sixty degrees if you live in the Black Hills of South Dakota. And, I'm one of the lucky ones.

Some are not so lucky. Some live where it remains cold throughout.

The Associated Press tells us at the close of this year (circa 2005) that a U.S. Census Bureau study reveals some bad news: Buffalo County in South Dakota, the home of the Crow Creek Sioux Tribal People (since 1863), has the "lowest median household income" *in the nation*, and that at least "twenty percent of the population have lived below the poverty line for at least thirty years."

Having been born there in 1930, raised there through adulthood, and being a tribal landowner there, I am of the opinion that the people there have lived below the poverty line much longer than a mere thirty years! My childhood was spent there sixty/seventy years ago, living in substandard housing (a one-room tar-papered shack with a dirt floor, to be specific) without electricity and water, taking part in the inferior educational systems offered to Indians, with loving parents and grandparents who had no jobs, no transportation, no money, and only their legacy of flawed hope to pass on to their children.

There are two questions that come to mind when one looks at the Census Bureau study referenced above. The first question is: **What are the real causes of this endemic and ubiquitous poverty?** This is not an idle question but one that has never been answered honestly or satisfactorily by the people who are in charge of Indian lives. As an example of the flawed rationale that accompanies this question, white economists (and even some Indian economists) tell us that places like Buffalo County are places "where there really isn't any economic development going on." Oh, really? The Crow Creek Indian Reservation, which lies along the east side of the Great Missouri River, is one of the seven Reservations in South Dakota that forfeited 550 square miles of treaty-protected Indian lands for hydropower in the Northern Plains 45 years ago!! What is hydropower development if it isn't economic development? The idea that there is no economic development going on is false. It's just that Indian Tribal governments and Indian peoples have been exempted from participation in such development through the implementation of a racist federal Indian policy collaborating with a state governmental system in order to enrich themselves and their white constituencies by stealing the resources of the tribes and then blaming the victims.

It is not a new tactic. Historians can tell us that the most significant Indian land-theft case in the United States (known in the vernacular as the precedent-setting "Black Hills case") was a nineteenth-century event that assured this endemic poverty talked of here. The Crow Creek Indians were signatories to the 1868 Treaty of Fort Laramie, a law of the land agreement that reserved their homelands after years of war. Within ten years of that agreement, they were witness to the theft of 7.7 million acres by the U.S. Congress. Thus, they were not surprised when the Congress later passed the "Allotment Act," reducing what was left of their land holdings by two-thirds, nor were they surprised when the BIA assisted the Department of Interior in ignoring the Winters Doctrine, trashing clear terms of the law again as they flooded 550 square miles of Indian treaty—protected lands in 1950 for hydropower in the Midwest. Why poverty? The answer is simple: an invading government cannot steal a native people's land and then ask why they are poor! No one in his or her right mind can presume that after such massive land thefts Indians will not be impoverished.

It doesn't take an economist to know that the consequence of land theft and water development in America has devastated Indian Tribes for most of the twentieth century. Tribal governments and tribal peoples have always been cut out of any kind of equal participation in the particularly broad development of water economies by federal/state policy that for hundreds of years has suggested that Indians must not be allowed to participate in the economic development of non-Indian economies. It was Helen Hunt Jackson who identified this particular white man's "ethic" concerning economies back in 1881 when she wrote this rationale taken verbatim from an 1838 report from the Indian Bureau giving instructions to commissioners:

> The Government has all along been suffering in mind from two conflicting desires ... "the desire to give these Indians an equivalent for their possessions," and on the other hand, "the well-ascertained fact that no greater curse can be inflicted on a tribe so little civilized as the Sioux than to have large sums of money coming to them as annuities."
>
> On the whole, the commissioner says that we are called on "as a matter of humanity and duty toward this helpless race, to make every exertion in our power NOT to place much money at their discretion."

Thus, treaty annuities were withheld, Indians lost land and starved, and the U.S. government wrote in its reports then and still does today that it continues to act "justly and generously" toward Indians. In further rationale, Jackson tells us in her historical and political narrative, "the record of the massacres of Indian peoples of that summer is scarcely equaled in the history of Indian Wars." And you thought Wounded Knee was the only one? On the contrary, there were hundreds. This scenario played itself out not only at the Crow Creek, but all across the continent and is the foundation for the prevailing relationship one sees today on all Indian Reservations.

Why recount this history if what we are focusing on is poverty in 2005? The reason is simply because we must contemplate what the consequences of thirty years, or forty, or fifty years (or a century) of poverty and political discrimination are to a tribe, a people, a community. What are the consequences of such a history? The consequences are before us: Indians are the poorest, least well-educated people in the United States not by accident nor by their own perfidy or mismanagement, but by the racist ideology and philosophy that have accompanied them from the first contact and earliest treaty.

Most reasonable economists and sociologists can assume that such racist and discriminatory policies as have been briefly described here cripple and damage people at every level of existence, mentally, physically, psychologically, politically. Jonathan Kozol, a twentieth-century public policy expert, has exposed the crime of racism and class perpetuated by the United States over and over in his work, most notably in two books, *Death at an Early Age*, and *The Shame of a Nation*. In these books he doesn't take up Indian matters, per se, rather, he takes up the matters that he says must concern the United States as it deals with its nonwhite and other isolated populations.

Kozol is not a ready companion of those economists who simply talk of poverty problems "in non metro areas," or in suburban areas "outside metropolitan areas," or "the wage gap in rural states," or "population growth," or "red v. blue states" and fail to mention the dreaded word *racism*. He suggests they are all missing the point that must be made and he is not alone when he suggests that Racism is at the core of discriminatory problems and endemic long-term poverty.

The poverty problems that face Indians reveal that charge has substance. For example, the water development spoken of here is particularly revealing. Hundreds of thousands of acres of treaty-protected Indian lands and many towns, including the place where I was born and raised, are under water. Yet white towns that were situated along the river were spared. Bismarck, North Dakota, Pierre, which is the capital of South Dakota, Chamberlain, just fifteen miles from the inundated Agency town of the Crow Creek Sioux, were all untouched.

These towns have flourished and are now destination tourist places raking in thousands of dollars, while many of the little Indian towns along that same route no longer exist. Isolated Indian communities have failing casinos run by criminal lobbyists out of Washington, D.C., and many of the Reservation economies are so bad their governments, like the tribal government at Fort Thompson, are facing "receivership" status. This means that the Bureau of Indian Affairs, that selfsame federal mechanism that has made utterly bad decisions for the tribes since the 1800s, will take over their governing functions.

What this means is that it is not only a decent job and a living wage, good health care, a useful education, and a thriving economy at stake. The very SOVEREIGN rights of indigenous nations are disappearing because of this massive poverty, and the possibility of that awful and final calamity brings up the second set of questions to be asked by Indians in these circumstances: **How do we move beyond rage to progressive political debate? How do we become participants** in the economic development of the region and deny the pockets of white wealth their greedy spoils? How can we reverse the results of two hundred years of economic discrimination?

The answers to those questions loom large. Social justice in an age of uncertainty should connect politics, pedagogy, and ethics to reasonable action in the world. The current generation of critical, interpretive thought and inquiry concerning Race Relations, Indigenous Rights, Economics, and Politics must move Indian tribal nations and their citizens beyond colonial and racist tactics, beyond futile questions, beyond being destroyed, drowned out, removed, and divided with only Bingo Palaces and Tourist Patios to put them further in the debt of those who would displace them and steal their assets.

First, even economists and policymakers must recognize crime when they see it, and force a recognition of what has gone wrong, not for the purpose of apology or reconciliation but for the purpose of putting in place a massive "Marshall plan" for returning lands and resources, rebuilding economies, government and legal institutions, and educational facilities on Indian Reservations. Indian tribal nations and their governmental institutions are in a crisis situation and are at risk of massive failure unless tribes can collect on their stolen resources to rebuild. Instead of casino debt and the paying of taxes to greedy state governments, tribal nations must restore their lands, their farming and horse- and cattle-raising economies, and must develop their energy resources such as reclaiming their water, as well as instituting such energy development as Wind Power Development. No more hog feeding, which pollutes water aquifers, no more digging coal, which destroys clean air, no more mining of uranium and making yellow cake, which pollutes the land and pays for the nuclear options of U.S. colonial adventures in the Middle East and elsewhere.

Tribes must do their own planning for the future of their own resource development, and do it in the context of their own cultures and histories. They must resist the market mentality and brainwashing of bureaucrats who bring forth one ill-conceived project after another. Tribes must somehow throw off the philosophy that we are "helpless," to be advised and sanctioned by the incompetents from Washington, D.C., and state houses throughout the country. The failure of the Consortium of Energy Resource Tribes, which began some decades ago, must be taken into account and we must start over. To start over we must develop native political leadership, and strengthen the frail Reservation-based institutions in government, law, and education that are facing disasters of immense proportions. We must admit to ourselves and to the outside world that tribal governments are presently in a crisis and the major cause for that crisis is relentless poverty brought about by colonial, racist political malfeasance at the federal and state levels.

In Defense of Politics and Ethical Criticism

The study of ethics, by its very nature, is the impetus for the political development of Indian Studies, yet we offer no specific course in it, as far as I can determine. There is nothing unusual about that academic reality, since there are few rigorous courses in "ethics" required in civics or law or mathematics, either.

My interest in ethics has focused on the examination of the connections between the art or profession of writing about Indians and the politics of the artist or writer. I've wanted to undertake the study of the general nature of morals and the specific moral choices to be made by the individual in his or her relationship with others, which is at the heart of almost any discipline studied in universities across the globe. In addition, I've been concerned with the rules or standards governing the conduct of the members of a profession, which are said to be vital in curricular design throughout academia and sometimes even in law schools, though those enclaves seem to me to be particularly loathe to delve into anything "philosophic" when teaching students how to "decide" cases and "litigate." I once heard a judge respond to my challenge at the bench by saying, "Well, my dear, it may not be right, but it's THE LAW!!!"

Allowing for the intrusion of ambiguity in the law takes a bit more than courage and good intentions, so the study of law is of particular concern to those who want to discuss right and/or wrong, justice and/ or discrimination. *Ethics* is usually defined as the study of principles of right or good conduct, or the study of a body of such principles. Many fear such studies border on "religion" and interfere with the parsing of every word so necessary in legal studies. To get too entangled in

186

that dialogue, they say, would mean that we would never get anything decided upon. While nearly everyone would agree that universities have the obligation to assist students in learning how to lead ethical, fulfilling lives, there continues the disagreement about whether or not the focus for studying ethics or developing ethical criticism in Indian Studies should be given deference considering the political nature of the discipline.

Most of the stuff you read about in ethics has to do with what may be called "constructing a life philosophy," which entirely misses the points to be made, one supposes, in the political/racial discussion of Indian Studies. How does coping with the struggles of constructing a life philosophy prepare anyone, let alone university undergraduates, for the nightmare of trying to understand the politics and/or morality of sacred sites, Kennewick Man, federal Indian policy, or the casino business?

In a techie world where nothing is true (neither is it untrue) until you've got it on your Blackberry, a discussion of ethics is a decidedly demoralizing undertaking. These days, when war is a matter of "first strike," education comes down to the mindless testing of sixth graders, the economy has ended up in the cosmos, and race relations, which make people turn on each other, are as bad as they've ever been in our history, the term *ethics* can find for itself no place to hide, yet, at the same time, no place to find the light.

Facing off in such a broad terrain, it might be best for me to limit my thoughts here to "ethics in writing" because I have been examining for much of my career the connections between writing about Indians and the rules or standards governing the conduct of the members of the writing profession as well as other academic professions. Ethical standards in such contexts have everything to do with history, some will say, and that fact makes the conversation we might have very unsatisfactory. For people who know nothing of a particular tribe's life history and life ways, almost everything that is said on behalf of the tribe often seems so idiosyncratic as to be incomprehensible.

In the long run, it is the relationship of the individual with others, after all, that is the subject matter of ethics, the moral choices and the general nature of morals the individual brings to group consensus. It was Rigoberta Menchu, who was involved most significantly in the ethics of self-representation, who said that not only is it an individual and private matter, *it is the truthfulness of that individual assessment of behavior* that brings about an authenticity of claimed identity and, thus, public responsibility. Her suggestion is that the critical analysis given by writers and thinkers on any and all subjects is essential to the development of a continuing tribal ethos.

We know what a scandal Menchu stirred up among the scholars who want to focus on "truthfulness" to the near exclusion of identity and/or the effects of dispossession. This has largely been the dilemma in writing about American Indians and is, perhaps, the reason we, with the exception of our colleague Vine Deloria, have not moved into a larger, more significant realm of prose and political scholarship as it pertains to ethics.

We all recognize that the dreadful poverty of Indian enclaves throughout the hemisphere, and the degraded status of those who are the victims of it, bears upon the tribal ethos in a fundamental way, which means that for those of us who are teachers and thinkers and writers, it is like looking into a vast abyss and we want to throw up our hands because of the daunting nature of it. What we have learned over the years, however, is that politics and morality meet at every level of the civilized condition. One does not exist without the other. What many political writers, including myself, have come to realize is that the political incapacity we see in the governments that surround us, as well as the endemic poverty of our people today and in the past, rises out of inadequate schooling. Morality does, too.

The improvement of the schools at every level, then, is the first and final concern. If that is not our first and final concern, then, the questions "Why write?" "Why teach?" need not be asked.

Acknowledgments

Some of the poems here are testamentary, conversational, not mystical, but a blend of narrative and elegy. Some pages of these poems won a Weldon Kees award in semifinalist category in April 2004. They are: "The Inadequacy of Literary Art," "In This," "Birds, Yellow Jackets, the Sun, and an Old Man," "The Old Couple," "A Mixed Marriage," "A Gentle Heart," "Going Away," "Murder at the Nebraska Line," "Change," "Exile," "In the Summer," "The Way It Is," "Restless Spirit," "While Watching a Prairie Bird," "The Morning World Is Like This," and "Dakota Iapi Tewahi(n)da." (To honor Kees's name, The Weldon Kees Award has been established by The Backwaters Press.)

The random nature of this collection illustrates the haphazard use of poetry, story, and nonfiction to illustrate how literary genres, unlike the samples of scientific experimentation, can form a coherent whole. Or, for those who require a more organized thought pattern, it can simply illustrate the unsystematic way an indigenous political writer keeps from going mad.

Notes on Sources

"When we talk of"

Cook-Lynn, Elizabeth. *The Power of Horses and Other Stories.* University of Arizona Press, 2006. The extract beginning *"Wic'a ak'i'uhan pi* is a constellation" is from a manuscript for a forthcoming collection.

"Hearing Spiders Pray..."

Barnes, Jim. *A Season of Loss.* Purdue University Press, 1985.

"Who Owns the Past?"

Gates is a notable scholar and professor of African American Studies. "Naipaul's Fallacy" is a reference to the East Indian writer's controversial influence in trying to say that all so-called minority literatures are fundamentally the same as European literatures, a stance that is in marked contrast to what is theorized in the study of indigenous literatures.

"Thoughts While Driving across a Bridge on Interstate 90"

Mni Watu is a Dakota Sioux water figure who gives them disease and death even today. Ikce is the first Dakotah, a word with a vast array of meanings, sometimes in the vernacular even translated as "face." Mythically, it is profoundly meaningful. When the ice breaks up in the spring, old Dakotahs say "Ikce is here." Shunk and Pahin are the dog and porcupine, both of primordial significance.

"Another Place to Walk Back From"

The novella *Roads* has been submitted for publication.

"Reading Guide to *Aurelia*"

This previously unpublished reading guide to my book *Aurelia* (The University Press of Colorado, 2002) is meant for teachers of literatures.

"What I Really Said . . ."

This address was prepared for the UCLA American Indian Graduation services held on campus May 17, 2004, to honor the Masters of Arts Candidates in American Indian Studies. The theme was "Remembering Our Roots While Discovering Our Futures," and a former student of mine from ASU was one of the honorees. Cook-Lynn, Elizabeth. "My Previous Life." In *I Remember the Fallen Trees*, Eastern Washington University Press, 1998.

"When I did graduate work"

Evans, David Allen. "Old Racquetball Player." In *Hanging Out with the Crows*, BkMk Press, University of Missouri-Kansas City, 1991.

"Whatever Happened to D'Arcy McNickle?"

This essay appears in an unpublished collection tentatively called *New Indians, Old Wars*. Reference is made here to James Wood's review essay in *The New Republic*, July 24, 2000, called "Human, All Too Human: The Smallness of the 'Big' Novel." I also wish to acknowledge the inspiration of a talk by Wole Soyinka presented on the campus of the University of Nevada, Reno, that same year.

"Murder at the Nebraska Line"

This poem refers to the unsolved murders, on June 6, 1999, of two Oglala men, Hard Heart and Black Elk, signaling the dozens of violent deaths (murders) of Indian people on the homelands that remain unsolved.

"Change"

This 1888 photo appears in many historical volumes, such as *Dakota Panorama* (edited by J. Leonard Jennewein and Jane Boorman, Dakota Territorial Centennial Commission, 1961). This photo is one of many that record the colonial pressure being put upon tribal leadership to accept the Allotment Act to break up tribal treaty lands, an Act that was resisted by Sitting Bull, who stands off to the side, and many others. It is said that Sitting Bull left this gathering for home, got on his horse, and visited every Indian Reservation in the territory, urging the leaders to say no to the notion of allotment. He was shot to death two years later by the U.S. Colonial Police, standing in the top row of this photo, just two weeks before nearly 300 Minneconjous were murdered by the Army at Wounded Knee Creek.

"October 2004"

Momaday, as a major spokesperson for Indian cultures and literatures, was addressing a college audience in Portland, Oregon, during the 2004 Lewis and Clark quincentennial in the United States when these remarks were made.

"Exile"

Wole Soyinka lived in Abeokuta, Nigeria, when he won the Nobel Prize for Literature. As his writings excoriated the corruption of African dictators, he was no longer safe from violence in his homeland. He has since been living in the United States and teaching in several elite universities here. He is one of the most important Third World writers of our time.

"The condition"

Sommer, Dorris. "No Secrets." In *The Real Thing.* Edited by G. M. Gugelberger, Duke University Press, 1996.

"There are few vocations"

Gass, William H. *Finding A Form.* Knopf, 1996.

"Phyllis Schlafly says this:"

Brock, David. *The Republication Noise Machine.* Crown, 1998. Or see *Questions of Free Thought and Religion* at www.atheism.about.com (last accessed May 22, 2006).

"Below the Poverty Line"

Jackson, Helen Hunt. *A Century of Dishonor.* Harpers & Bros., 1881. This classic in Indian Studies was a stunning exposé of government malfeasance. "Poverty In Indian Country" was previously published in the December 15, 2005, issue of *The Lakota Journal* (Flandreau and Rapid City, SD).

About the Author

Elizabeth Cook-Lynn, one of the writers of the twentieth-century Native American Literary Renaissance, is the author of three novellas, *From the River's Edge, Circle of Dancers,* and *In the Presence of River Gods,* which were published as a trilogy in *Aurelia;* two poetry chapbooks, *Then Badger Said This* and *Seek the House of Relatives;* a full-length book of selected and new poems, *I Remember the Fallen Trees;* and a nonfiction work, *The Politics of Hallowed Ground: Wounded Knee and the Struggle for Indian Sovereignty,* coauthored with Lakota attorney Mario Gonzalez. Her collection of essays, *Why I Can't Read Wallace Stegner and Other Essays: A Tribal Voice,* was awarded the Myers Center Award for the Study of Human Rights in North America in 1997.

Cook-Lynn is a member of the Crow Creek Sioux Tribe, Fort Thompson, and lives in the Black Hills of South Dakota. She is a recipient of an Oyate Igluwitaya award given by native university students in South Dakota, an award that refers to those who "aid in the ability of the people to see clearly in the company of each other." Since her retirement from Eastern Washington University, she has been a visiting professor and consultant in Native American Studies at the University of California, Davis, and at Arizona State University in Tempe, and a writer-in-residence at several universities.